Thurber, TX, mid-way between Fort Worth and Abilene, had an abundant coal supply and this helped open up the Southwest when railroads began expanding westward.

Digging coal was hellishly hard work, but an opportunity for thousands of immigrants from the "Old Country." There were amenities: housing for $6.00 month, a happy, musical city with an Opera House, a dozen bands, concerts, dance pavilions, lavish holiday parades, beauty pageants and swimming at Little Lake and a semi-pro baseball team. A city with no unemployment, no taxes, no politics, very little crime and $2.00 a month for family health care.

The ancestral relatives of the ex-Thurberites are scattered all over the United States. But there still remains an affectionate THURBER CONNECTION where interesting events and personal experiences are often relived.

THE THURBER CONNECTION

LEO S. BIELINSKI

Thurber Historical Association
Box 192
Gordon, TX 76453

THE THURBER CONNECTION

First Printing by Thurber Historical Association 2008

ISBN 0-9638476-1-9

ISBN 0-9638476-1-9

9 780963 847614

THE THURBER CONNECTION
TABLE OF CONTENTS

THE THURBER CONNECTION
TABLE OF ILLUSTRATIONS & PHOTOS

FOREWORD

There are perhaps 200,000 people scattered throughout America who have ancestral ties to Thurber. This is the "Thurber Diaspora." When Thurber was shutting down from 1921 to 1933, 3,500 people had to relocate. The majority of Thurber's coal miners moved to the Illinois coal fields. Others went to the potash mines in New Mexico. Some went to California where there were a variety of job opportunities. Many chose to remain in nearby Thurber Junction (Mingus) because they owned homes and sustenance was from bootlegging. Those connected with Thurber's oil operations moved to Fort Worth offices or to other T P Oil Co. locations in Texas. It should also be emphasized that throughout Thurber's coal mining years (1888-1926) workers and families "came and went" when they could not adapt to the hard labor of the coal mines.

The result of all this scattering has been that "no telling when you'll run into somebody who knows about Thurber." This is called "The Thurber Connection" and hence, the title of the book. Today, folks who actually lived in Thurber are becoming scarce, and it's usually recalling grandparents or uncles who lived in Thurber. Anywhere in America and in particular, the Fort Worth area, one is liable to make a "Thurber Connection", and there is unanimity in the fondness of recalling Thurber; for Thurber provided an opportunity for a better way of life. Although a company town, Thurber had good living conditions and there was always "something going on." When Johnny Biondini's family moved from Thurber to Grant's Town (Mingus) just a mere quarter mile north, it was like moving to a whole new world. In Thurber there was electricity, running water and gas heat. In the Biondini's Grant's Town home there was a big adjustment to coal oil lamps, well water and wood burning stoves.

There were 16 different nationalities in Thurber; mostly Eastern European with Italians comprising over half the coal miners. The Italians were colorful with their singing and happy disposition. And they were a significant force in Thurber's unionization. Not often mentioned in the literature is that Thurber had two United Mine Worker Locals, the original 1903 Local and the Italian Local; the latter being granted three years after the first Local.

Thurber was a completely unionized company town with "Service from Cradle to Grave." If you worked in Thurber you belonged to a union. Here was a modern city with no unemployment, no taxes, no politics, medical care for the family at $2.00 a month and very little crime.

There is much literature on Thurber, but unfortunately, the firsthand accounts will soon be nonexistent. And there are writers who have never visited Thurber or even talked to an ex-Thurberite but references are cited and twisted to fit imaginations on how Thurber should have been. "The Thurber Connection" tries to set the record straight by presenting narrations from a variety of sources and various aspects and events in Thurber's colorful past.

Leo S. Bielinski Ph. D.
August 2008

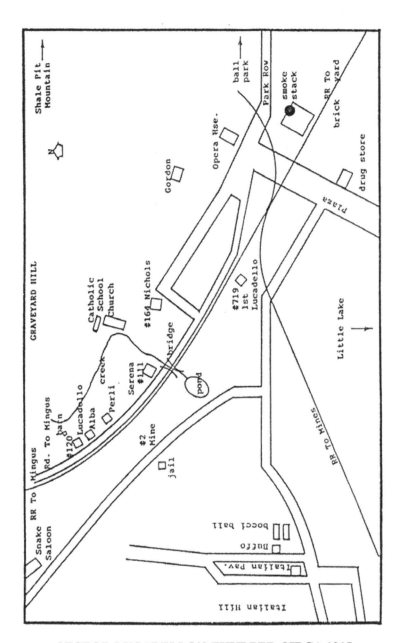

VICTOR LUCADELLO'S THURBER CIRCA 1915

vi

VICTOR LUCADELLO'S THURBER

Edited from Victor Lucadello's 1990 Manuscript

It is amazing that after seventy years Victor Lucadello's Thurber experiences remained so vivid he was able to recall and write fifty-some pages. His story is about an Italian kid growing up in Thurber and his personal touch makes delightful reading.

Of great interest are Victor's comments on gardening in Thurber. Some writers on Thurber (who probably have never been to Thurber), authoritatively proclaim Thurber was rocky and covered with shale from the mines; therefore, nothing would grow in Thurber. But the valley between Italian and Graveyard Hill where Victor lived, and most other locations, had good fertile soil, and people were able to grow almost anything.

If you look at "Lucadello's Valley" today, you will see the slag dump from #2 Mine, the old jail ruins, the foundation of the Snake Saloon, the RR track bed to Thurber Junction (Mingus) and grazing cows. But the pond, the bridge (their hangout) and the creek, all such a big part of Lucadello's youth, are not discernible, wiped out by highway construction.

Victor Lucadello last visited Thurber in 1981. He passed on before he could make another visit to Thurber.

This is a story of a Texas coal town and its people whose past is more intriguing than fiction, a story that must be preserved because society forgets much too soon. It was in this coal town where a dozen or more European and native cultures met and merged with the harshness of the early west to form perhaps the most unique community in all America.

1

"Give me your tired, your poor," reads the inscription at the base of the Statue of Liberty. And so they came teeming into the environment of early Thurber. Miners from the "Old Country": Italians, Poles, Slavs, French, Irish, Germans, Scots, English and Chinese gave a racial mixture which Texas had never seen. They came, each with his own dream of a better way of life for himself and his family.

Halfway between Fort Worth and Abilene on Texas Interstate 20, the motorist will see a few weathered brick buildings and a tall brick smoke stack, rising 126 feet above the highway, standing as a sentinel guarding Thurber's past. A service station replica of a coal mine tipple is there. Next to the service station is a burned-out shell of a two-story brick building, formerly the town's drugstore, where Ucho, Monkey and I would sometimes go for an ice cream cone, soda or a candy bar.

Within a radius of one mile, scars on the landscape indicate the former locations of homes and buildings where 10,000 people once lived. This was Thurber, the town of our birth, and once the largest city between Fort Worth and El Paso.

Dago, Polack, Nigger, Hey Boy, Hunky, Wop, Grease Ball, Chili Picker, Bohunk and Chink were some of the racial slurs I heard. But most of the above had the experience of working with a pick or shovel. Papa had that experience when he first began working for John Barnadon Construction Company of St. Louis in 1923 after the coal mines in Thurber closed down. In fact, a few of the Italian immigrants who returned back to their homeland, after their stint in the U.S.A., took back to their villages the picks or shovels they had used, to show family and paisanni what kind of work they did in America.

MIGRATING TO AMERICA From what I remember of hearing our elders talking in Thurber, Worden, Illinois and in Roseland, a Chicago suburb on the south side, it was Natale Dalbello, his wife Milia, and their son Milio who were the first of Mama and Papa's friends to migrate to Thurber. And it was through them that Papa, Pasqualle and Pagnian left the village of their birth in 1904 with high hopes of a better way of life than the one they had in Italy. On arriving in Genoa, the three young men, including many more of their generation, boarded one of the many ships used in taking hundreds of thousands of immigrants to the Promised Land, America.

After arriving at Ellis Island, it took a few days of thorough examination before they were permitted to go on to their destination, Thurber, Texas. And although they knew hardly a word of English, they somehow managed to send a telegram to their friend Natale, to let him know when they would arrive in Thurber Junction (Mingus). When they arrive in Fort Worth, they were transferred to the Texas and Pacific Railroad which was owned by the railroad tycoon, Jay Gould. An hour and a half later they arrived in Thurber Junction.

On the morning of their arrival, Natale, with the help of Pietro Serena, hitched up his mules and drove the one and a half miles to Thurber Junction (Mingus). Having arrived about an hour before the train's arrival, Pietro suggested they have a beer at Goebel's Saloon which was a couple hundred yards east of the depot, saying, "Natale, avemo piude una ora prima che riva el treno, andiamo dentro la osteria de la Goebel's, e bevone un per birra." ("We have an hour's time before the train's arrival, let's go to Goebel's Saloon and have a couple of beers.") "Va Bene" ("Very good") was the response. So, after downing their schooner of beer, they ordered a second, then helped themselves to beef sandwiches at the end of the bar, which went with the beer.

They were about to order another beer when they heard the whistle of the coal-fired steam locomotive. They rushed out to the depot, and a few minutes later, three very happy young men stepped off the train to be greeted and embraced with great joy by Natale and Pietro, welcoming them to a new life in the land of dreams.

It was no wonder then, that there was great rejoicing, hugging and kissing, Italian-style, of course. Joy, happiness and excitement was at its height, all of them grateful and exultant for each other. The nodding of their heads, the movement of hands and waving of the arms as gestures of understanding, is indeed, an Italian's beloved tradition.

After the great joy of seeing each other again, Pietro picked up their bags and tossed them into the wagon. With this done, Pietro again nodded his head towards the saloon saying, "Venite con mi, e adiamo a questa osteria e se mangiano uno patetino inbuto, con carne de mango, e ancha un per de bicerri de birra." ("Come with me, we'll go into this saloon and have a couple of beers and also a beef sandwich.") The five happy Italians walked up to the bar, ordered their schooner of beer, quickly downed that, then ordered a second beer and helped themselves to the sandwiches. Since the new arrivals were on the hungry side, they had a second sandwich, then walked out and climbed into the wagon which would take them to their new home on "Italian Hill," which the natives called "Dago Hill." Natale began the trip back to Thurber, passing through Grant's Town which was adjacent to Thurber. On arriving at Thurber's Plaza, Natale drove his team through the main business district, which in turn led them to the only road that would take them up the hill and to their final destination.

This road was bedded down with slate and slag that was taken out of the coal mines. The road ran parallel to the railroad tracks up to the top of the Hill, but the railroad went farther west to various mines, some of which were about five miles from the town plaza.

THURBER RECEPTION   While Natale and Pietro Serena were gone to Thurber Junction to greet the new arrivals, Buffo, with plenty of help, had set up the newcomer's reception in the new Italian Pavilion which the Company built after the Union contract in 1903. All buildings and houses in Thurber were owned by the company.

Buffo, father of Joe and Tony, had built a couple of bocci courts where many of the Italians, including those living in the valley, would gather to play that all-Italian game of bocci, to play cards of Italian origin, or the Italian finger game, or talk about their coal digging, their families here and those left behind in their villages and their hopes and dreams of a life in America.

The Buffo house was the second house north of the road leading to Italian Hill, and when Natale reached the top level of the Hill, he first pointed to the Buffo house, and then pointed to the new Pavilion saying, "Varde! Ha e la cassa de Buffo, e la via e el novo pavilion dove tutti i nostri amicci spetono per ti con bracci operti."("Look! There is the house of Buffo, and over there is the new pavilion, where all our friends are waiting to welcome the new arrivals.") Quite a few families and bachelors brought some goodies for the happy occasion: salami, sopresse, sausages, spaghetti, cheese and plenty of outside-oven-baked bread. Some brought homemade wine and grappa (whisky) while others chipped in for a keg of beer. My future Godfather, Bostiano Bartolo, played the accordion for dancing and singing.

After Natale pointed out the Pavilion where the reception and celebration was being held to welcome the three young men to their new home on Italian Hill, he drove to the boarding house he and Milia were keeping. After they were settled in a room with two other boarders, Tony and Guido, the happy newcomers were escorted to the Pavilion where they met others whom they had known in Italy.

And what a happy and joyful occasion it was for Domeni (future Papa), Pasqualle and Pagnian with the warm welcome the new arrivals received from their fellow countrymen. The welcoming celebration lasted until after midnight (tomorrow was another workday) and the Dalbelos, their son Milio, their boarders Tony and Guido and the three newcomers, walked back to the boarding house which was to be Papa's home for the next two years when he married and moved into a house nearer downtown.

It was in the newly-built Pavilion (nicknamed "The Bearcat") where the Italians held all their celebrations: weddings, holidays, parties and Saturday night dances. There was another dance pavilion downtown, a hundred yards east of the Opera House. The Mexicans also had their dance pavilion.

Many Italians in Thurber were musically talented. The town had several bands, but the "Hunter Band" which was comprised of mostly Italian musicians was the "official" Thurber band. And this band played at the Dallas Fair and the Fort Worth Fat Stock Show.

GETTING SETTLED IN THURBER   The Italian immigrants who came to Thurber, the town of my birth, usually ended up on Italian Hill, one of the five hills which surrounded the town. This was a natural tendency to gather with those of your own culture and language. With their bread, good food, wine, bocci and animated talk, the Italians were the most colorful and populous of Thurber's people. And they became better known than other nationalities.

There was Italian Hill, Polander Hill, Stump Hill (Mexicans), Graveyard Hill and New York Hill where the oil workers settled after 1918. And these hills formed a little valley on the north side of Thurber, and this valley was where I grew up and had many wonderful experiences.

Shortly after Mama and Papa married in 1906, they moved into House #719, which was not on Italian Hill but near downtown, a hundred yards northwest of the grocery store. Their family continued to grow and in 1913 they moved into House #120 which was near abandoned #2 Mine. This was a good move because the house had four rooms and not too many houses around us. But the best part, as far as Papa was concerned, was the three or more acres of fenced-in land, a barn, chicken coop and pigpen. Next to the pigpen was our outhouse and next to the house, the shed in which Mama used to wash clothes and Papa to wash grime from his body (no bathtub) after a day's work in a mine. He used it until the Union made the Company furnish washing facilities for the miners. And, of course, we kids used the washtub too, for our baths. Inside was a monkey stove, just like the one we have here in Kenosha, and this was used to heat the water needed for the above doings.

The kitchen was where we ate and entertained no living room like today. A few chairs and benches served the seating purposes for eating, playing cards, or mora, the Italian finger game which the men enjoyed, sometimes winding up in a very loud argument almost to the point of fighting.

In one corner of the kitchen was Mama's icebox. A large cooking stove was at the other end of the room. It was made of cast iron, and when the winter months came around, it would turn red-hot, and if you pressed a pencil or a piece of wood against it, it would instantly burst into flames. And if you spit on the top of the stove, the spit would hop around like ping-pong balls. But the tub of warmth coming out of that stove really felt good to us as we sat around it.

Next to the kitchen was Mama's and Papa's bedroom and in the other room was an iron bed which Marie, Neta and I shared. Also in our room were stored bags of flour, sugar, cornmeal for polenta-making, salt, coffee and a twenty-five pound box of crackers which was really handy for the small folks. From our front porch facing the valley, we could see the town's jail and the slag dump of the old abandoned #2 Mine. A road which led to Strawn was cut through the slag dump, and fifty feet east of the dump was the Texas and Pacific RR to Thurber Junction (Mingus). Some fifty feet west of the lowest end of the dump was the town's jail, in which Papa had spent one day of a 30-day sentence for getting caught making booze in 1920.

LUCADELLO'S VALLEY   When we moved to the east side of the valley next to Alba's family in 1913, I became the best of friends with Ucho and Monkey (Victor) Serena, especially with Monkey because he was a couple of years older than Ucho and me. The Alba family, going south to the town square, lived next to us. Next to the Alba family lived the Perli family, followed by Perli's married daughter Antonetta, then two more Italian families. And next, just across the wooden railroad bridge (under this bridge was our hangout) in House #111, lived my best pals, Ucho and Monkey Serena. Next to Ucho's house was our church and school. Next to Dalbelo's house lived a mixture of Italians, Mexicans and Irish. And in the first house next to the church yard (I remember going there a few times with Ucho and Monkey), lived the Nichols family: Manny, Dahl, Faye and Sadie. Going north from our house towards Grant Town were four more house in which lived a mixture of Italians and Mexicans.

Some thirty feet west of the railroad bridge was a small pond about seven or eight feet deep, which always provided the water for the creek, which meandered under the wood bridge (our hangout), around the Serena House and field, around the school yard, then turned north towards Grant Town. This source of water was a "Godsend" to those who were lucky enough to live along the creek.

Some fifty feet behind our barn was the creek from which Papa got water for his animals and garden. Between the barn and the creek was a huge oak tree where Papa put up a swing for his young brood in which we had lots of fun. Across the creek at the base of Graveyard Hill, Papa planted his grape plants. There was an assortment of trees, including some mesquite trees which made mesquite beans which we kids liked and which Papa used a few times to make moonshine.

Next to the wash shed was our garden which provided our needs for various vegetables such as potatoes, tomatoes, cabbage, beans, lettuce etc. These were stored in a storm cellar that Papa had built during his time off from the mine, and also where he kept his wine, sopresse, salami and garden produce for later use. He also built Mama an outside bake oven and also added another section to the back part of our barn, where he stored bales of hay, and where he and Mama made moonshine. At first the moonshine was for their own use, but when the mines began to close, for the oil workers around the Ranger area after W.K. Gordon struck oil there.

It was in this house and valley that I got to know Ucho and Monkey and where I spent (although too few) the best years of my childhood. The Ponsetti and Bottini families were also settled on the east side of the valley when we moved there. Rose Ponsetti worked in the Post Office and Joe worked in the mines until he was drafted in the WWI Army.

1918 FLU EPIDEMIC   The Pent family sold popcorn just outside the movie house and lived at the west end of the Snake Saloon, facing the road which went to Strawn. It was Pee Wee Pent's father who was in charge of the booze which was stored in the saloon's warehouse after Palo Pinto County went dry. And when the flu hit our area in 1918, much of the whiskey stored in the warehouse was used by the company doctors as medicine for those who were hit by the "bug". Many people died during that period.

I remember the lines of men, women and children, including our family, lined up at the doctor's office getting vaccinated. It must have been a blessing on our family because none of us was sick from that killer flu that I can recall.

I remember in my early childhood, our boarders nicknamed me "Nino" (short for Victtorino). That name stuck with me until I shifted to Chicago looking for work in the spring of 1929.

Some of my earliest recollections at a young age remain with me in my mind in the form of pictures. Such as Mama singing her many Italian songs as she went about doing her work outside, boiling clothes on the outdoor fireplace, scrubbing them, rinsing them, then hanging them out to dry. Making bread, pedaling her sewing machine and many other pictures associated with our Mama.

PLACES WE EXPLORED IN THURBER   Italian, Polander, New York, Stump and Graveyard Hills surrounded the town of our birth. Then there was Big Lake, Little Lake, Palo Pinto Creek, Barton's Creek, the Brick Plant, slag dumps of the abandoned mines and the old swimming hole near the Shale Pit. These places made exciting and fascinating surroundings for the exploring youngsters of Thurber.

The abandoned mines and their slag dumps were ideal for exploring. Of course, there was always the danger of getting hurt, but thanks to our "Protector," no casualties occurred. Our young legs came to good use as we climbed to the top of the mine dumps and hills to look down into the valley and saw the lakes, brickyard, the 128-foot smokestack, the different church steeples and the hundreds of homes in which 10,000 people lived. And the center of this sight was the home of the Gordon family. It was a lovely two-story house laid out on a three acre plot of well-landscaped terrain.

The creek in the back of our barn was where we had so much fun splashing water at each other and trying to swim in two feet of water, but we were mud crawling. Going for crayfish (we called them craw dads) in the creek. Getting the common mushroom in our field, the Alba field and in the school yard after a good rain. The fishing and swimming hole which came into being as a result of digging out the shale used to make the famous Thurber Bricks. The Little Lake had a pier with a diving tower, but what we kids enjoyed the most at Little Lake were the water carnivals with the various races, diving contests, and sometimes, a beauty contest was held. The Big Lake was a private club for the executives of the Company. Stump Hill was where Company personnel played golf and where many tournaments were held. It was there, too, where Ucho, Monkey and I would go looking for lost balls which we would sell for pennies, nickels and dimes, then we'd go to the drugstore, managed by an over-seven-foot-tall man whose name was Weeks according to Jim Ponsetti.

The first ballpark was on Graveyard Hill, east of the Graveyard. New York Hill was where the oil people lived after they struck oil in Ranger in 1917, fifteen miles west of Thurber. Up on New York Hill was where I helped my sister Marie clean houses. Many times Ucho, Monkey and I would go hunting for birds and small game with our slingshots in the fields and along Graveyard Hill. We really had some great fun. We had so much going for us to see and do in Thurber. But it all came to an end just four years after W.K. Gordon struck the "Oil Bonanza" near Ranger in 1917.

MOVIES   The kids of Thurber, like Ucho, Monkey and I, certainly enjoyed watching the silent movies. We would talk about what would happen to the good guys in next Saturday's afternoon matinee movies such as "Perils of Pauline", or the "Squaw Man" featuring silent film star William S. Hart. And there was Eddie Polo, Elmo Lincoln, Art Accord, Ken Maynard, Charlie Chaplin, Fatty Arbuckle,

Douglas Fairbanks and his wife Mary Pickford, Delores Del Rio, Ruth Roland, the Barrymores, Hal Roach, the Keystone Cops and many others.

It was at the movies where the youngsters of our town gathered on Saturday afternoon for the matinee performance which always left us in suspense until the next episode of the serial, so very popular way back then.

While the pianist was adjusting her music to the mood of the pictures appearing on the screen, the projectionist operated the machine which threw on the pictures and the printed words which were silently spoken by the different characters. Ushers saw to it that none of us kids made a noise which would distract the attention of the other viewers of the melodrama or comedy being shown.

However, today's audience accustomed to radio and television, may look at these early entertainments as objects of mirth. But back in those days there were many people who purchased season tickets to make sure they could attend the above.

ITALIAN CULTURE   The Italian immigrants implanted their cultures in their new settlement. There, they built another "Little Italy", something like "Dago Hill" in St. Louis. They planted their vineyards and fruit trees, built their outside bake ovens, their bocci ball courts and their cellars to store their wines, salami, sopresse, cheese and produce. They had learned early in life the need of being thrifty and they conserved anything of value, and this characteristic served them well in this land of plenty. But as a whole, the Italians in their newfound colony on the Hill were happy and contented. All had everything in common; their needs were simple, and if any one of them were in need of a helping hand, it was given without question.

Old Man Buffo had built a couple of bocci ball courts where many Italians gathered to play that Italian game of bocci. Living nearby and knowing his sons Joe and Tony, I would go there often.

Some Italians had trouble learning the hard-to-understand language of America, not because they didn't want to, but because most of them had very little, education in their homeland village.

CATHOLIC SCHOOL   As an example, when Marie and I first started going to Thurber's Catholic School, Hunter Academy, in the fall of 1915, we knew very few words of English, but we certainly could speak the dialect of the Hill as if we were born in Italy, the only language spoken by our elders.

Back in those early days there was no law which required children to attend school until the age of sixteen. Some boys dropped out of school after a few years to work in the mines. However, the Sisters had night school if these boys wanted to learn. There were no Child Labor Laws then.

Mother Superior and the Sisters of the Incarnate Word of San Antonio in Thurber's Catholic school were strict disciplinarians who did not believe in spoiling the child by sparing the rod. They allowed no squirming, whispering, rubber band spit ball slinging, moving around in class, or any other unruly behavior. I suppose one could say children were regimented in those days. They were expected to line up in orderly fashion when marching in and out of the school building.

They looked like gentle nuns. But if you dropped out of line just a little bit, they would yell out loud and clear enough to make you jump. And if any of the 400-500 kids got smart-alecky, they would really come down on you, but hard. They would whack hands, knuckles or your behind, but good, with that bumblebee killer paddle. We certainly knew that it didn't pay to get far out of line.

Mother Superior had a withering look that could quell the most bumptious boy. When a defiant brat told one of the Sisters in front of all the students that she had treated him unfairly, she made him walk up front, bend over and gave him a half dozen whacks on his backside with that bumble bee paddle they always kept handy, all the while, telling him loud and clear, so all could hear: "Obedience comes before all."

In case you don't know, a bumble bee paddle is a quarter-inch thick piece of wood shaped like a tennis racket with ¼ inch holes drilled into the face to allow air to pass through. And as kids in Thurber, and also in Worden, Illinois, we made and used them to do battle with the bumble bees when we went looking for their honey hives. And many were the times we got a stinger into us from those angry, fighting bumble bees.

Sometimes they built their hives in the ground and also in the hollow of trees, and although we would get a stinger on our face, neck or arms, when the battle was over, we enjoyed the honey, and if it was an extra large hive, we would take it home. It was indeed a lot of excitement, expectation, and most importantly, the fun we had. The swelling caused by the stinger would cause some pain, but by the time the swelling receded we were ready to do battle again.

These gentle-looking nuns and Mother Superior ran the school like a well-oiled clock. There was no monkey business while you were under their care. And you know what? It did most of us a lot of good. They believed in discipline, and they certainly made us walk the chalk line.

Although the school was on the tough side, their theory was that all children needed to be taught a sense of value. The best way they saw it was through strong discipline. They believed in teaching lovingly, but when it came to discipline, they put all their faith in strictness. Amen.

Each morning we entered our room, stood to attention until the sister teaching us walked in, whacked the wall with her bumble bee paddle and looked us over. And always a "Good Morning, Children," "Good Morning, Sister." Then she'd begin the "Our Father," and we'd recite this prayer.

Here is a song I still remember singing quite often some 65 years ago: *It's always fair weather, When friends get together, In work, or in play, It's a wonderful day.*

MEDICINE SHOWS   Near the warehouse of the Snake Saloon was a wide open lot which was used for medicine men shows which popular back were then. They sold medicines which they claimed would cure most anything. I remember one in particular when Ucho, Monkey and I were there watching. An elephant was part of the show. There was a ten or twelve-foot wooden bridge over passing a small creek. The bridge, as it turned out, was not strong enough for the weight of the elephant, so down he goes in about three feet of water. The elephant was not hurt, but the medicine man had to dish out the money to repair it. It wasn't funny to the medicine man, but it was to many of us who were watching the elephant as he crossed the bridge.

A PEEK AT A DEAD MAN   I, and I'm sure Ucho will too, remember the day he and I went fishing with our cane poles at Little Lake. It was on the hot side, and the fish just weren't biting, so after a few hours, we gave up and took a short cut to get home by going through the west end of the town square. A block past the pool hall and the bowling alley was the white frame building of the company's undertaker. When we got near the building, we noticed that the front door was wide open. Being curious, we looked in and there in the center of the room was a dead man stark naked lying on a table. I'll always remember the cuts and bruises he had. You could see the coal dust imbedded in parts of the body wounds; he was hit bad. A loud voice came from the back yelling, "What the hell you damn kids doing here?" Boy! Did we take off, scared to death! We were about a quarter-mile from home, but I'll bet that was the fastest quarter mile Ucho and I ever ran!

WALKING EVERYWHERE   Walking was a big part of my life then, but that was another day and time. Those days and times are no more, but I can assure you the memories still hang on, and will continue to remind me of those long-ago times when I was a kid growing up in Thurber. It's a different kind of life we are living today. When I was growing up in Thurber and later in Worden, Illinois, walking was a way of life. But walking today, except in malls, has become rare. Most people don't walk unless they really have to. Yet, what pleasure they miss. We walked everywhere: to school, to church, to funerals, downtown, uptown, in good weather or bad, day or night, and we met people walking everywhere.

On balmy spring days, we walked the countryside. We trudged muddy roads. Across meadows, into the cool shade of the woods, and we saw violets, daisies, trilliums and Jack in the Box. In summer, barefooted, we walked out in the countryside, the dust on the road sifting between our toes as we walked. When the creek behind our barn was shallow, we waded in the water, combing over the rocks looking for craw dads. Sometimes we cooked them in tin cans over an open fire. And when the day was coming to an end, we walked home barefoot in the glow of the setting sun.

In autumn, through the countryside and the hills, ablaze with gold, scarlet and russet, we walked through the woods, gathering pecans, hickory nuts, black walnuts, blackberries, mesquite beans, and then homeward bound with our loot. When I began to date (this was back in Chicago), I walked to my date's house. The two of us walked down Michigan Avenue in Roseland to a movie at the Roseland Theatre, or to old St. Anthony's Church basement in Bumtown, Kensington Avenue, to dance. Sometimes we'd go to White Castle at 11100 and State Street for their delicious hamburgers and a soda or coffee. Then I'd walk her home, then walk myself home, thinking of the nice time we had.

LIVERY STABLE   The people of Thurber had many things going for them in the form of recreation. The Company had a livery stable where one could hire a horse and buggy and take his sweetheart out for a Sunday afternoon ride in the countryside, drive to the different coal mines, to Big Lake or Little Lake, Barton's Creek, to Mingus, Gordon, Strawn or the cotton fields, or many other places of interest around our area. There was a sign hanging in front of the livery stable with the following words on it: "You like something to drink in hot weather? So does your horse. The whip is merely an ornament and not to be used on our horses and don't drive to kill, you may want to hire him again someday." Our town, with the open saloons and other forms of entertainment, had the reputation of being a rough town. It was a Mecca that enticed many young men from surrounding towns and areas.

BASEBALL   Thurber had one of the finest semi-pro baseball teams in Texas and played in the "Oil Belt League." The games were very popular and drew large crowds at the Sunday afternoon games. Ucho, Monkey and I would often go to see them play.

The first ball park was on Graveyard Hill, but the second ball park was east of town on Park Row, about three-quarters of a mile from our house. It had seats for about 1,000 spectators and was enclosed with an eight-foot -tall board fence.

BUTCHERING   While working on this manuscript, I came across the word "purselane" in the dictionary. We called it "pusly weed." I hadn't thought of the pusly weed since I was a kid in Thurber. It grew mostly in and around gardens, but it also grew wherever the animals grazed. And when I was nine or ten, Mama gave me the job of feeding the pigs. Twice a week I would gather the weed and mix it with the other slop they ate, and fatten them up getting ready for the kill, when Papa and a few of his paisans pooled together to make salami, sopresse and sausages.

The pusly weed had fleshy, succulent leaves when they first grew up in early spring. They were very tender and Mama would use them for a salad. Later she would use them for pickling and garnishing, but for the most part, we fed them to our pigs.

It was the Alba, Dalbelo, Serena and Perli families who pooled together when it was time for butchering. Each man had his job: turning the manual meat grinder, cutting the pieces to size, feeding the hopper, packing the casings by punching the casings of sopresse and salami to the desired size, then hanging them in the basement to drain and cure. The women prepared the food and anything else the men needed in their work.

The day began early in the morning and as they worked, they imbibed: wine, coffee with homemade grappa (whiskey), smoking their corncob pipes. Petri or De Nonli Italian cigars, then chewing the butt that was left, spitting on the floor as they worked, and by the time they were through, the area in which they worked, which was the kitchen and porch, was a slippery mess. It took the women well into the night before the area of work was somewhat back to normal.

MAKING WINE   When the wine season came around, the Texas and Pacific RR would sidetrack a few boxcars of California white and red grapes at the Thurber Junction (Mingus) siding. The wine makers of Thurber would drive teams of mules or horses to Mingus and buy as many cases of grapes each needed, and Papa was no exception.

Papa would dump a few boxes of grapes in a wine barrel which he had cut in half, and we kids would get in barefooted and stomp on the grapes and eat some of the grapes as we squashed them into juice. It was a fun day for the kids.

Papa always made at least three barrels of wine for his own use. And then when he was through, he would make a barrel of what is called "second wine", which was just wine-flavored water for his young brood. But to us kids it tasted better than the water that was delivered to us by the mule-driven water wagon.

PHILOSOPHIZING   Who, you say, would find excitement in Thurber? But wait, look! Here the rains fall, the sun warms, the seed pushes its way through "Mother Earth", and the green leaves uncurl. This then is the message of life. This is how it was, is now, and shall forever be, world without end.

I remember the sassafras shrubs in our area. They were easily identified by their small flowers of pale yellow, and the spicy taste and fragrance of green leaves, twigs and bark. Our Mama would use sassafras to make tea by boiling the root bark and also use the oil of sassafras to perfume the soap she made out of lard and lye. It wasn't until we moved to Worden, Illinois before I knew there was soap other than the kind Mama made.

Life goes on; everything that is, was. And everything that was, will be. A year follows another year, a decade follows another decade, a century follows another century, the rebirth continues, and everything comes back to life.

This then is the miracle. There is no death; there is, in truth, eternal life. And with the coming of spring, we plunge our shovel deep into the garden plot, turn under the dark, rich soil, rake fine the crumbling clods, and carefully press the inert seeds into orderly rows.

The spring blooms whispered the way into summer marigolds, canna and fancy leveled colodurnas. Autumn brings chrysanthemums followed by flamboyant poinsettia, peonies, bleeding heart and many other winter blooms. Scattered among the seasonal joys were year round displays of roses, iris and phlox. It was no wonder then, that the townspeople, and many far and wide, called Thurber a wonderful place. Springs were not always the same. In some years March, or sometimes April would burst upon Thurber's hills and valley in one miraculous leap, all of nature's things trying to get its share. In some years, spring tiptoed in, came forward then paused, as if overcome by shyness, peeped in, then ducked out of sight. And sometimes it was off center, but it never failed to work its wonders. The trees leafed overnight, all dormant things awakened; marigolds, roses and baby iris came forth as the earth warmed. You can feel it, you can smell it, and then crumble the earth of April in your hands. A warm wind slowly moves the various forms of clouds in the gentle skies. The rains come, good rains to sleep by, and the fields that were once done as a plug of Brown mule chewing tobacco, turns to a pale green, then into the brilliant green of life, reminding one of a theme like a beautiful, haunting melody, its message a mystery.

BLACKBIRDS   I'll always recall the blast of guns two or three times a year after we moved into the valley. Papa, Natale, DeBosc (my Godfather), Perli, Serena and the Alba's hunted the beautiful red-winged blackbirds, halfway up Graveyard Hill, around 6:30 in the evening. That's about the time the red-wings would come lying over the hill heading for Big Lake where there were plenty of cattails to roost on and water to drink.

Every evening about the same time, the red-wings would come flying over Graveyard Hill in flocks of thousands. It seemed to me that a huge, dark cloud suddenly appeared and came over our heads, shutting off the light, covering us in darkness.

All of us were prepared for the blast of the guns, from which the black birds had no defense. Mothers and their children were ready with baskets, bags and pails. The first dark cloud came flying over the hill, right on schedule. The men ready, then the loud booms of the shotguns, followed by the echoes coming back from the surrounding hills. It lasted about twenty seconds the first time, and then after reloading, about fifteen seconds the second time. But it sounded like all hell had broken loose as the red-wings were on their way down to the waiting women and children. But it wasn't until the sun began to set, that the search for the red-wings came to an end. After we were through searching and picking up the birds, we all gathered at the Alba family's back yard. While the rest of us defeathered the birds, Vecha Alba, Milia and Mama dressed them. Sometimes over 500 red-wings were shot down. This was repeated three times yearly. And then followed the fiesta. Women prepared the birds, chickens, pieces of pork with a variety of spices. The men would set the barbeque cooker and carefully put in all the meat the women had prepared. Beer, wine, and homemade grappa (whiskey) for the ponchini. Soda and second wine for the kids. We kids had to keep dousing the meat with the sauces and rotate the cooker. We had so much fun at these gatherings, enjoying a good feast. Ucho, Monkey and I would cop a bottle of good Dago red wine and a few bottles of beer, and this would make us feel contented and sleepy.

W. K. Gordon, the "Bigga' Boss" of our wonderful town, pitched in some shells and did some red-wing shooting. Everyone knew he loved to hunt birds and enjoyed eating them. In the 30s Gordon drilled a few wildcat wells around Gordon, Texas. On his visits to Gordon he always stopped at the John Harlin Grocery Store for fresh butter, eggs and pork sausage. He was fond of wild game and Mrs. Ralph Finch of Gordon who operated a cafe at the "Y", east of Gordon, said that Mr. Gordon frequently brought her dressed blackbirds for her to bake a "blackbird pie." He would pick up the pies on his way back to Fort Worth.

RABBIT HUNTING   We fished a lot and hunted for all kinds of game: rabbits and quail and doves. It was in the fall of 1918 when Ucho's older brother, Pietro, took Ucho and me hunting for rabbits, Pietro taking his dog Blacky with us. Pietro had his 10-gauge single barrel shotgun. Ucho and I had a single shot 22 rifle which Papa let me use at times. Mama was watching us until we were out of sight as we headed for the north end of Graveyard Hill. After we were out of Mama's sight, I begged Pietro to let me try his shotgun He reluctantly agreed and carefully showed me how it worked, warning me, "It kicks like a mule." But this did not deter me.

It was but a few minutes until Blacky had scared up a jack rabbit and began barking as he hightailed it after the jack rabbit. Pietro knew that the rabbit would come back to where he had started, so we waited for the rabbit to return with Blacky on the rabbit's tail. The barking became louder and louder, closer and closer. Finally we saw the jack running straight towards us with Blacky barking and in hot pursuit. I lifted the big gun to my shoulder, pulled back the hammer, aimed towards the rabbit and fired. The next thing I knew I was flat on my back, and the gun had fallen from my hands. Indeed, I felt as if I had been kicked by one of Papa's ornery mules. I was laying flat on my rear end while Pietro and my good friend were laughing as if it were a fiesta of some kind. Believe me; I didn't think it was so funny. I was still on the ground and I asked, "Did I get him?" "Yes, Nino, you slowed him down some, and then Blacky caught up with him." Blacky shook the rabbit a few times, and then came to Pietro with the rabbit as if Blacky were saying, "OK. He's yours." Although I was hurting and my shoulder was beginning to swell, I was well pleased and satisfied with myself for having the nerve to shoot the "Big Gun."

Pietro took the rabbit (an old jack) and took his hunting knife to cut through the tendons of the rabbit, then wrapped the belt and Jack around my belly. And as we were walking home, the front feet dragged the ground; either the rabbit was too big, or I wasn't too tall.

When we got to our barn, Pietro hung the rabbit on the side of the barn and skinned and gutted him. He cut the rabbit from the head straight down. He kept half and gave Mama the other half which we ate at the following supper. We had stewed rabbit, formai freet, and Papa gave us a glass of his better wine to wash it down.

CHURCH   Most of the Thurberites were religious minded and most of us attended church on Sunday. On Sunday Thurber was not obscured by the murky clouds of smoke, and the sun poured down its yellow radiance, and this had a tranquilizing effect. The mines, brickyard, the ice house, in fact, all of Thurber's industries were at a standstill on Sunday. The ringing of different church bells called the flocks to the fold. The greetings of friends on the church grounds. Then the ringing of church bells again when services were over, and once again people would gather in small groups to discuss the past week about their work, their ills, joys and sorrows while the youngsters tromped, ran and played until their elders were ready to go home. It was, indeed, a Sunday tradition for most of Thurber's 10,000 people. And on our way home after church, we looked forward to the Sunday dinner, a meal of some importance. Sometimes friends would come to visit, the men to play cards of Italian origin, while having their coffee, grappa, beer and homemade wine. The women talked among themselves, and the kids played outside.

Italians, Mexicans, Poles, Irish, Germans and a few English attended St. Barbara's. It was located at the bottom of Graveyard Hill on the southwest side. It was run by Father DeLuca and the Sisters of the Incarnate Word, consisting of about ten or twelve nuns.

Mama and Papa were married in this church, we were all Baptized in this church, and seven years later Marie and I began going to school there. It was moved to Mingus in 1936. (St. Barbara's was moved back home to Thurber in 1993.)

When Pina and I went to the Thurber Reunion (which has been held yearly since 1937), on June 13, 14 and 15, 1981, we went to Mingus to see the church and to take a few pictures. It sure looked so much smaller than when we were kids and played pussy-in-the-corner at the base of the church bell.

MAMA'S THRIFTINESS   Mama was a very thrifty person and she used the leaves of dandelions in salads, boiled the tougher leaves with other vegetables and roasted the roots to make a drink similar to coffee. The blossoms were crushed for wine making, as did their parents in Italy.

It was after we had moved into the valley, and Papa built a hen house, that Mama had a yard full of many-colored chickens and at least a half-dozen hogs. And she made countless trips to the creek carrying back buckets of water for the pigs and chickens so that she had worn a smooth path from the creek to the pigpen. I remember her talking to herself, saying, "Doppo quella bestia de animale e andatto dentro la cabbia de la galine, nainca una de le galine va dentro la cabbia e adesso mi tocca vardare per tutto a cattare i ove." ("Ever since that doggone raccoon got into the hen house, not one of my hens will set foot into the hen house, and now I have to hunt all over the place to find the eggs.")

CHICKEN FIGHTS   The Mexicans of Thurber had plenty of excitement when they held their rooster fights at some location, known only to them. Much money would be bet on their fighting roosters, equipped with razor-sharp knives (gaffs) attached just above their spurs. The men would gather in about a twenty-foot circle. Only the ones who were fighting their roosters were allowed in the roped circle. The fight would continue until one of the fighters was killed.

THE MESQUITE TREE   The mesquite tree was valued for its bean pods, which are pulpy and sugary. It is also called honey mesquite. At that time, there was a vague belief among some of the Mexicans that after death, their souls would enter into the mesquite that fed them such good beans during life.

The mesquite tree has very long, sharp pointed thorns. When Pina and I drove to Thurber in 1981 to attend the Reunion, I brought back a small branch and a root of the mesquite tree and also a stone. These I picked up as I walked up the hill on the rocky road that would take me to the cemetery. As a youngster, I remember being pricked many times in picking the beans. We would pick them before they dropped to the ground. We ate our fill, then would take the rest home and lay them out to dry. They were very sweet and enjoyed by the kids, including some of the elders. Papa used them to make moonshine sometimes, mixed with the grapes from his vineyard. Sometimes I ate so many beans I would become constipated. Our toilet was the outhouse which had two holes cut out for a person to sit on. Then there was a lower hole for the "small fries" such as me. I never liked going inside to "do my things" because of my fear for the wasps. It seemed to me they always built their nests in our outhouse. Anyway, I remember having to go a few times after eating too many beans and being constipated. The fear of the wasps and not being able to "go" made me call to Mama for help.

HOT SUMMER DAYS   I recall the sometimes real-hot days of summer, the sun slashing down like an acetylene torch with heat waves and mirages dancing gaily around, so you could never be certain that what you thought you saw was really there. A certain hill had the mystifying habit of making one see double on certain days, shivering greatly before disappearing from view. The air was bone dry and clear, and the only limits of vision were the curves of the earth and the dancing terrain. The heat, for one thing, didn't make you feel miserable, even though its intensity gave you the feeling of a fresh-baked loaf of Italian bread like Mama baked, just taken out of the oven. The air was so dry that it soaked up sweat quickly, serving a dual purpose. It gave you an aura of evaporating moisture for cooling and your lungs felt fine and pure. You knew no germs could survive in the air, and once your eyes got used to the glare, there were all sorts of fascinating colors and places all around the horizon to feast your eyes upon.

MY FRIENDS UCHO AND MONKEY   It was after Marie and I began going to Catholic School that I got to know Ucho and Monkey (Victorrio) who would become my best friends. Victorrio got the name Monkey because of his facial expressions. When he was born, his left hand and arm were half the size of his right arm and hand. And when he grew older (he was fourteen when we moved to Worden, Illinois), his arm looked like the arm of a five or six-year-old. He was like a big brother to me. It was Monkey who made me my first beany (slingshot); Ucho and I were seven at the time. Later he taught us how to make our own out of a bike's inner tube, a piece of leather from the tongue of a worn-out shoe, the fork from the branch of a tree, and some of the twine Papa used to tie up salami and sopresse. The beany was our first weapon to hunt birds and small game, which we did along the creek, our pastures, the school yard and the base of Graveyard Hill. Later, when we began to get better at hitting small targets, we began using marbles (we called them mibs), and covering more territory by taking the railroad spur coming in from Thurber Junction (Mingus), past the Snake Saloon and to R.A. Rutherford's on the Back Road to Thurber.

We would take along a forked branch of a tree, about four-feet long, just in case we ran into any rattlesnakes or copperheads which we sometimes did. One of us would nail the snake to the ground with our fork and end his poisonous time on this earth.

STUBBORN DONKEY MUSSO   It was in 1917 that I overheard the following story while watching the men folks play bocci ball at the Buffo courts.

Pietro Serena, thirty years old and the older brother of Ucho and Monkey, would take his jackass named Musso, to the woods, gather up firewood and load it on Musso's back. Walking alongside of his jackass, he proceeded on his way home. Halfway home, Musso made up his mind that he wasn't going any farther, that Pietro had overloaded him for the last time. So Musso sat himself down on his backside and there he was going to stay. Pietro tried everything: coaxing, even begging and using his belt, but to no avail. Pietro was at his wit's end when his friend Aldo Perli came walking by, carrying a basket of vegetables he was going to give to a paison of his. Pietro said, "Aldo, I have done everything I know to make this stupid Musso move, but he will not budge!" "Well," said Aldo. "I think I can be of help." With that he reaches into his basket, pulls out one of those red-hot Mexican peppers and said, "Here, Pietro, take this pepper; break it into two pieces and shove one piece up Musso's cullo" (butt). "Oh gracia, gracia, tanto!" he replies and did exactly as Aldo had told him. It wasn't but a split second until Musso got up on all fours, his eyes rolling, his ears and tail straight up and lets out a couple of loud "hee-haws" and took off running full speed down the road. Pietro turned to Aldo with an amazed look on his face, "Aldo, Aldo what can I do now? I will never be able to catch Musso now!" Aldo, looking at Pietro with a self-satisfied look on his face said, "Oh, yes you can. Take the other half of the pepper and shove it up your butt; I'm sure you'll catch up with your stupid Musso!"

OTHER THURBER ITALIAN FARMERS   During the watermelon season he (name not given) and one of his daughters would come to Thurber with a load of watermelons, both red and yellow meaters and made his rounds. His first stops were in the valley, then to the Negro section. His next stop was on Italian Hill where he would put his wagon near the pavilion. He would ring his bell and in a few hours he would be sold out. Mama always got two or three, and being a good friend of Mama and Papa, he always gave her an extra one. Believe me; we sure enjoyed these, especially the yellow meaters because they were sweeter than the red meat.

There was another Italian farmer (Companella?) whose farm was located on Gibson Branch, north of the Big Lake. When Papa took his family to the Companella farm we would spend most of the day helping to gather the various vegetables they grew, most of which he would sell to the two Company stores, one on the square and one on Polander Hill. After having supper, our folks would sit outside and talk, mostly about their relatives and friends in their villages back in the Old Country. Maria and I would cross the road that came from Thurber, climb the high bank of the Big Lake, and when we got to the top, we looked at the huge body of water and would say something about how the water got there. Companella would give our parents a variety of vegetables to take which Mama put to good use.

THE BIG LAKE DAM BREAKS IN 1919   The Thurber Big Lake was built about a mile southeast of Thurber in 1896. It was Hunter's private fishing and hunting club and Thurber's water supply, covering 100 acres. It was built to replace the Little Lake because Thurber quickly outgrew the water supply from the Little Lake. The Little Lake was located a couple-hundred yards south of the Town Square. It was raining hard when Papa left home to catch the "Black Diamond" train in the Town Square that would take him to the coal mine. It was still a steady, hard rain as Marie, Netta and I had breakfast, as we had to go to school.

Mama, when looking out of our kitchen window, saw that the water was overrunning the creek and heading to the barn, pigpen and chicken house. She called us to help her rescue the eleven piglets in the pigpen. We rushed out and managed to pick them all up, putting some of them in Mama's apron. We then splashed our way as far as Mama's bake oven, trying to get to the chickens. But the water was really rising fast by now and was carrying away the chickens that failed to get to the higher roosting place which was in the chicken house farther down stream. We could no nothing for them: too late.

We went back into the house, cold and soaking wet (it was January), soaking from top to bottom. At its peak the water reached up to the floor of our front porch. But our outside storm cellar, where Papa kept his wine, sopresse, salami, produce and jarred food, got about a foot of water, which we bailed out after the flood receded with very little damage. It was like one big lake, reaching all the way to Thurber Junction. A large oak tree on the dam was uprooted by the force of the water where the dam gave way and landed about where Highway I-20 runs now.

Besides all the debris scattered throughout the valley, bass, catfish, crappie, bream and perch poured out with the water and were picked up by many of the people living in the valley, including us and people living in Grant Town and Mingus.

No school that day: too much clean-up to do at home, although some of the kids did report, but were sent home by the nuns. Our school and church, on a higher ground at the base of Graveyard Hill, was not affected except for some debris in the lower section of the school grounds, near the creek, which was cleaned up the following day by the school kids. Although we, like others living in the valley, did lose quite a few chickens, we did manage to save our baby piglets.

No one was hurt, not even Papa's friend Companella whose farm was below the lake dam, except for a few acres of winter wheat he had planted in the lower section of his property. The house, barn, outbuildings and equipment were on higher ground so there wasn't any damage. But it did leave a lot of cleanup for the people living in the valley.

The day of the dam break, rumors were strong that it was the Little Lake dam which gave way. We were all relieved later in the day to hear it was the Big Lake and not the Little Lake, as the public school was near the Little Lake's twenty-foot dam, as well as many homes. For certain, had it been the Little Lake, the homes nearest the dam would have been demolished by the force of the water and many people, including children, would have been killed or injured.

Within a couple weeks the dam was reconstructed, and when we visited Thurber in 1981, the Lake had been made into a fishing-camping resort with cabins and clubhouse etc. The Company rushed sandbags, equipment, lumber and sixty men to salvage as much of the Lake as possible. But before it came under control, more than two-thirds of the 100 acres of lake water had poured all the way to Thurber Junction.

NEW YORK HILL   In 1918 the Company built about thirty new homes for the white-collar workers who had come to Thurber to administer the oil bonanza W. K. Gordon had hit in nearby Ranger. The houses were built on a hill more south than east of the Town Square and was given the name of New York Hill, because many of the people came from New York. Each house, some two-story, was surrounded by a picket fence, nothing like the miners' houses; much more expensive. A brick sidewalk ran all the way from downtown, up the hill and to the houses. And brick sidewalks led to the entrance of each house which had well-landscaped yards with grass, shade trees and shrubbery of various kinds, bordered by beds of brightly-colored flowers – and the latest in indoor plumbing. It was on this Hill and in Gordon's home at the end of the Town Square that I first became acquainted with indoor toilets, instead of the outhouse. Believe me, it certainly was a big improvement over going outside in the winter cold, and there weren't yellow jacket wasps to contend with.

SOME ITALIAN NAMES I REMEMBER Ponsetti, Pent, Dalbelo, Gruppo, Nano Americo, Reginatto, Pasqualle, Pagnian, Alba, Serena, Biondi, Buffo, Dibosco, Bartolo, Andreatti, Bertino, Beneventi, Biondini, Bottini, Brunello, Castro, Crovetti, Companella, Fantin, Ferrero, Gazzalo, Garburo, Aria, Lorda, Margona, Marchioni, Meneghetti, Moleher, Piacentini, Pellizzari, Perli, Lee Americo, Revelto, Solignani, Santi, Zanetto, and Zinanni.

Joe Ponsetti's mother Clara was born in Bradentown, near Coal City, Illinois about sixty miles south of Joliet in 1869. His father was born in Italy in 1865. He migrated to the states in 1869. He first worked in the coal mines in Colorado where he met and married Clara. Their first son John was born in 1893 in one of the Colorado coal camps, and soon after they moved to Thurber. It was in Thurber that Clara gave birth to Mary in 1895, the mother of Tony Rossini's wife, Bella. After Mary, came Joe in 1889, followed by Jim in 1900. Then Rose in 1902 who worked in the Thurber Post Office. Last of Clara's brood was Frank (nicknamed "Ching"), in 1906. And when Thurber went to hell in 1921, the family moved to the coal mines in Southern Illinois around the Benton area.

I met up with the Ponsetti family when we moved in the Roseland area, a suburb on the south side of Chicago, in 1929. It was in Roseland that I also met many other Italians who had lived in Thurber, including the Bottini family, consisting of five children.

WORKING IN THE COAL MINES   The working day of the coal miner began at 5:30; that's when the whistle at the ice plant would blow.

While his wife was getting breakfast ready, the miner dressed for work. His clothing consisted of blue denim overalls, matching jumper of the same material, heavy work shoes and a heavy canvas coat for winter.

After having his breakfast, the miner got his lunch bucket and left for work. These lunch buckets were made of enamelware, shaped like a double boiler. The top part contained the noon meal, and the bottom half was used for the day's supply of drinking water. The miner would place his arm past the elbow through the pail's handle, and with his hand underneath the bucket; bring it to rest against his body. He simply carried it in an upright position under his arm which prevented liquids from being spilled. And many times the lunch pails served a dual purpose because some miners would stop at the saloon after getting off the train, and refill the water part with beer to take home and drink with their evening meal.

In winter, with the mine trains leaving for work before daybreak, each miner would light his carbide lamp before leaving home in order to light his way to the train. On his way to the train, he would usually stop in front of the house next door shouting, "It's time. Are you ready to come?" ("Le ora, settu pronto a venirri?") And together they made their way, picking up others as they walked towards the siding where the train was waiting. The hundreds of lights moving from all directions reminded one of fireflies in a swamp.

T & P Coal Company had bought several ancient passenger coaches from a railroad and converted them for use in taking miners to and from the mines. These wooden coaches were similar to those used in western movies, except that all the seats were removed and replaced with wooden benches which extended the entire length of the cars. Coal stoves were used for heating in cold weather, and in summer, all windows were opened. When they were no longer needed after the mines closed, the coaches were parked on a siding at the lumber yard until they were sold for salvage in 1930. As the miner opened the door and entered the coach, he was greeted by his coworkers through the blue haze of strong tobacco smoke; cigars and pipes were burning full blast. There, many friendships were made.

The train began its slow progress up Polander-Italian Hill as it moved towards the mines. The men who lived in the valley boarded the train at the Town Square. Another stop was made near the General Store on Polander Hill to pick up those miners who lived on Stump, Polander and Itallan Hills. Stops were then made at the mines which were still in operation (no more than four mines were open at one time). The coaches were then placed on a siding at the most distant mine which was about five miles from the Town Square, ready to be used for the return trip when the day's work was done.

After getting off the train at the mine he was assigned to, the miner would pick up his "checks" (metal discs bearing his number) from the board in the mine office, where they had been taken from the cars of coal he had mined the previous day. He then filled the bottom half of his dinner bucket with water from a nearby faucet, took his place in the line facing the mine shaft to wait his turn being lowered to the bottom. Upon reaching the bottom, he walked down the dimly-lit tunnels to his working room, ready to begin the day's work. But first, he carefully placed a piece of coal or slate on top of his lunch pail so the rats could not get to his lunch.

The T & P RR began converting to oil in 1913, and after reaching peak coal production in 1915, the demand for coal decreased so that the mines worked half the hours they did during the war. Some miners picked up extra cash making bootleg moonshine. In 1921, with the mines working two or three days a week, the Company canceled their contract with the UMW, which still had another year to run, and announced a reduction in the wage scale. The two locals (the English and the Italian) refused to accept the Company's wage scale and refused to work. Some families left Thurber to secure work elsewhere. And without income, families could not pay house rent, so the Company asked them to vacate. A "Tent City" was set up just inside Palo Pinto County and just outside Company property. These WWI Army supply tents were purchased by the Union to shelter the coal miner's families.

There was little violence during this Lockout. Thurber and Thurber Junction (Mingus) were armed camps because there was also a railroad strike going on at this time. Armed guards patrolled the railroad shop and yards in Thurber Junction. Scabs were protected by shotgun-carrying guards. And the scabs (some of them former union members) were hauled to and from New #3 and #10 mines which the Company operated until 1926.

Meanwhile the coal miners waited in vain for an agreement between the Union and the Company at the Southern Coal Operators Conference being held in Fort Worth. They had high hopes of being told they would be back working in the coal pits. And when they were told no agreement had been made, they could not believe they were no longer needed in the Thurber coal mines. As time wore on, they began to drift away. Many families moved their belongings in boxcars to the coal fields of southern Illinois around Taylorville and some to Collinsville. Papa and a few of his paisans moved to Worden, Illinois to work in the K.D. Mine. Many families moved to California to work in the grape-growing industry that was coming on in that state. A few families moved to other states to begin new careers in other fields. Those remaining in Thurber Junction, who owned their own homes, turned to bootlegging for a livelihood.

MY LAST DAYS IN THURBER   The summer of 1921 was the last summer that we would live the good life of my childhood in Thurber. Papa took me with him for the last time to hunt for doves around Shale Pit Mountain where they got the clay for Thurber bricks. It was about a half-mile east of town. The taking of the shale resulted in a large pond (more like a lake) long before we kids started going there. It was here that many of us learned to swim, and where we spent many hot days swimming and fishing. Although Little Lake was open to all towns people, this big clay pond was the favorite swimming hole of my growing up days in Thurber. We called it "Clay Hole" or the "Old Clay Pond." And when the water was too cold for skinny-dipping, we fished for catfish and sunnies (sunfish).

The pond had a long clay slide down a high sloping bank, and when it was wetted down, it became as slick as grease and this made for fancy show offs in many ways. Single, two-at-a-time slide, belly whopper, sitting up, head first or on our backs.

On the high banks of the pond, we spied distinctive flowers which looked like brownish-purple wisteria blossoms. We would scratch the damp soil and up would come a string of Indian Nuts, from ten to thirty in a row. Although they didn't look too appetizing, we would wash off the clay dirt. After washing off the dirt, and if there were a bunch of them, we'd take them home, and Mama would clean, boil and mash them and make them taste better than potatoes.

I really belong to that generation which marked the ending of a different way of life. I was twelve then, and during that handful of years, I witnessed the whole thing happen. I, my friends, my family and my generation were born in a world of hard work and necessary patience, patience for an opportunity for life in this great land of America. The name of the coal town of our birth still echoes with a kind of distant pathetic and mournful music, even sixty years after its demise. All of those who had worked in the coal mines have gone to their Maker. But their children, who are still living, remember. They still feel and hear the real human drama that went on in Thurber: the hardships, the joys and the groping for light among people born in darkness. The last days of my youth were also the last days of the town of our birth; a haven for the Italian immigrants and other immigrants who came to the coal town of Thurber at the turn of the century.

OPPORTUNITY IN THURBER'S COAL MINES

Digging coal in Thurber was a hellishly hard job. The 30 inch thick coal required digging from a prone position and miners had hip and shoulder pads sewn in their work clothes.

When the Johnson brothers started the first mine in 1886 the miners were Knights of Labor Union members who had come from the defunct Coalville Mines, six miles northeast of Thurber, or about three miles north of Gordon, Texas. But union wage demands soon put the Johnson mine in a financial bind.

When R. D. Hunter bought the Johnson coal enterprise in November 1888 he soon broke the Knights of Labor Union because he knew he could not operate profitably at union wages. And word was put out in other mining towns: "Avoid Thurber, non-union rules." And when American miners shunned Thurber, Hunter began recruiting Eastern European immigrants, mostly Italians and Poles, but 18 different nationalities in all. Without this hardworking, inexpensive labor force Thurber might not have prospered. Many miners saved and sent "passage money" back to the "Old Country" for brothers, nephews, and cousins to join them in Thurber.

Hunter paid $1.05 a ton (reduced to $1.00 in 1894), but he had the coal screened which cut the miners' output by 20%. Thus, working 10 hours a day, six days a week, a miner dug about 2 tons a day and would make about $40 a month.

Often overlooked is the fact that the women worked as hard as the men. To supplement the miners' meager pay, families took in boarders. For $18 a month a miner got a bunk bed, two daily meals and a work lunch and laundry. And the laundry was done with a boiling pot and washboard. All this was in addition to pregnancies and taking care of the small children. One family had 18 boarders.

Today it is hard to imagine how anyone could leave family and friends to migrate to a place of work under such harsh conditions in a strange country. But there was opportunity in Thurber, Texas; something which was totally lacking in many repressed European countries at this time.

For insight into the difficult life in Italy around 1900, and why Italians eagerly came to Thurber, the autobiographical notes of Lorenzo Sartore have been made available by his son Gino Sartore of Pittsburgh, PA. Lorenzo's notes give credence to the belief that most Italians have inherent musicality.

"The following is a reproduction of autobiographical notes made by Lorenzo Sartore while in Sarasota, FL between November 1984 and April 1985. This is a word for word reproduction with only minimum editing either in spelling, grammar, punctuation, etc. in order to preserve the exact sense of his comments."

(Signed) Gino Sartore (Lorenzo's son) November 1992

(A story by newspaper writer Jon McConal, gives an interesting follow-up to the experiences of Lorenzo's brother Giovanni, who worked in the Thurber coal mines and who is buried in the Thurber Cemetery.)

LORENZO SARTORE'S NOTES   1895...Year that my father passed away. I remember like a distant dream, the following – My father was a farmer. He together with my mother I remember used to work very hard leaving the house very early in the morning with a 4 wheel flat top cart drawn by two steer my father if front of the steers with along stick leading the steers leading them to one of the field to do the seeding the planting of wheat corn, etc. My mother following in back of the cart with a rake on her shoulder, was going to help my father they work very hard all day. only time for rest was under a shady tree to eat their meager lunches, they never returned home until dark very very tired. at the day the work was not yet finished for them. we had in the stable from six to eight milk cows and some calf. My mother used to prepare supper for us while my father had to feed the cows. milk the cows and clean the stable. by this time my mother had supper ready for us. we all sat and ate supper together. after supper we used to gather all in the stable especially in winter months. Note – the stable with all the animals was warm the only means we had to keep warm in the winter time. Around the stable there were benches where myself my brothers and my sisters used to sit and spend the time. my mother had a spinning wheel she used to make yarn. with this yarn she made bedsheets, towels and other linen necessary for us. before going to bed my mother used to gather all of us together and used to recite the rosary all together. My mother was a very religious person a beautiful person – May God bless her. My poor father die very young at the age of 47 years of age – only. I believe he die of pneumonia. When he die in the bed room there was lots of people a lady lifted me up to give a kiss to my poor father just before he die. My family consisted of 4 brothers and 3 sisters all very young. when my father die probably my oldest sister Giulia was working in the near by silk factory earning few penny a day. My brother John was also working in another nearby factory he also contribute his meager wagers to substain us and help ourmother the best they could – but no one in the family wanted to continue the work of the father. So my mother decide to sell all the live stock, farm equipment. the land was not a problem it was all rented farm and we did not own any land. My oldest brother decided to emigrate to North America, my mother decide to leave the farm altogether and with all of us kids went to live in the small town of Caselle in a two room apartment. My sisters Giulia, my sister Caterina and brother Giuseppe had a job working the factory, sister Paolina and myself used to go to the elementary school. brother Pietro about three years old was at home with the mother. –

A couple years later my sister Giulia got married with Pietro Doria a mechanic by profession – she had three children Maddalena, Nettina and Paolo. Around the year 1887-88 brother John asked brother Giuseppe to join him in America, and did send him the necessary money for brother Giuseppe to make the trip to the USA. brother John first he settle in Pennsylvania around the small town of Vandergrift, Apolla working in a coal mine, later on with some friend he moved went to live in the Texas coal mine town of Turber not in existence any more and started working in the Union Pacific RR coal mine. brother Joseph reached brother John in Turber Texas. After a couple of year together my two brother were planning to return home in Caselle Italy to live with mother and family. in Texas brother John was very much interested in music, he was playing the trombone in the band and teaching music in spare time. Music was his hobby – unfortunately brother John took sick unexpectedly and two days later he die, probably of peritonite. in the coal mine of TexasTurber where he worked there was no doctors and he had no medical aid he was only 25 years old. Brother Joseph he immediately return back to Italy. brought back with him the saving of Brother John. It was evident from the letter we received from brother John that Brother Joseph did not like to work in coal mine and his contribution to John's saving was not very much but at his return home he claimed half of the money for himself also the fifth of the other half of the money that brother John saved. When brother Joseph returned home it was decided with my mother to use this money to purchase a house situate at Grangiotti only few hundred yards from the house where I was born. with the house was also a piece of land a fruit orchard and a big garden for me to take care of. by this time I was probably 10 – 11 year old. Myself and sister paola going to school. We had a milk cow and sometime a calf that we sold to the local butcher bringing in some cash for my mother.

GIOVANNI SATORE IN 1900 "HUNTER BAND" UNIFORM

Brother Joseph & sister Caterina use to go to work in a factory. after school it was my duty to bring the cow to graze to feed the cow. Nearby every afternoon. This was one of my chore. After a couple of years my mother took sick and doctor recommend taking her to hospital in Torino, where she die unexpectedly. Impossible to describe how much we missed our mother. we were crying crying

crying all the time and for a long time but she was in heaven with god, never returned with us again. She was buried in Torino Cemetery. Not known to us where she was buried.

There is so much I could write about my mother. She was a wonderful person. She had lots friends. Everybody used to love her – she was 49 years old when she die. After mothers death brother Joseph got married with a girl name Maria Cubito. Two boys Felico and Norato were born. I was working in a spinning Mill when my mother die. I was 12 years old earning 12 cents per day working night turn 12 hours per night. earning barely enough to by bread for my self. I was living with my brother Giuseppe. later on we separate and was living with my two sisters Caterina & Paolina & Brother Pietro until I was about 14 years old. When I was about 13 years of age my brother Joseph bought me a 2d hand cornet and I began to study how to play it. after six month or so of practicing I was able to join the La Novella di Caselle band. that cornet was my past time my hobby. I was very happy also very proud to be the youngest member of the Caselle band.

My brother Giuseppe was also playing the tuba in the Caselle band at the time. At this point (14 years old) I began to realize that working the Mills at Caselle for the rest of my life was going to be a very miserable life so I figured that in order to improve my condition it was very important for me to learn some kind of a trade. In Caselle (Grangiotti) there was not much opportunity for me to learn a trade. so sister Paolina had a boy friend Toni Bergamasco was working in Torino. he was a mechanic working for FIAT Auto Work. I asked him to help me to find a job for me in Torino. Toni was finally able to find a job for me. one of his friend was a forman in a nuts and bolts factory where I finally got a job. Wages was very small and was a struggle to make enough money to support myself. But it was a start in the right direction. After some months I met some friend of mine riding the train from Torino to Caselle. one of them asked me what kind of work I was doing in Torino. I reply a Tornitore (lathe operator). The job I was performing was not exactly a tornio (lathe) was some kind of a screw machine makin screw but I was bragging a little bit, so this friend of mine say to me where I am working they are looking for lathe and Tornitori, why don't you come to look for a job where I work they are paying good wages money there – I took the advise and went to apply for a job at the Industrie Metallurgiche Torino. later on it became part of Fiat Auto Work. I was accepted and they put me to work on a real engine lathe. this machine was all new to me. The forman a kind old man showed me my locker and engine lathe, and a blue print with a casting on top of the blue print, and told me get started to work. He told me up there are a big pile of the casting, get the handy man bring them to you – this casting was part of a RR car to be machined according to the blue print.

I began to look at that lathe for a long time, maybe more than one hr did not know what to do with it finally the forman noticed that I was not getting started come over to me and sayd – why are not you getting started what is wrong with you? the first thing that came to my mind I sayd to him the lathe i was working on was much different than this one which was the truth. at this point I figured now the forman is going to fire me for sure. instead this old man started to show me how to run the lathe and was the beginning of my career. I did worked for the Industrie Metallurgiche for over five years. I learned to be a mechanic. Worked there until I was inducted in the army 1910 – I was 20 years old.

My military life 1910-1913

In those days in Italy the military service was compulsory at the age of twenty every able mail was called to 2 year service in the Army. the class of 1890 was called to service all over Italy but for some reason the city Caselle was not called for about forty some day later for the reason I found out later Caselle was considered a zone having an infectious diseases but anyway one Sunday evening my brother in law came over my house to advise me that the carabinieri were looking for me with the notice that the following day I was supposed to present myself in person at the Torrino military Center District.

Some friend of mine (musician in the Caselle band) told me that there was a maestro a Military Sergeant that needed some musician to form a Military band for the Regiment of RR Engineers of Torino, for me to go and talk to him since I was playing the cornet he could use me in his band. when I was inducted in the Military service, so myself with a friend of mine I find out where I could find and meet this maestro and we had a meeting with him. he took my name and promised to do all he could to get me in his RR Engineers Service. I was so happy to think that I was so fortunate to serve my military time in Torino near my relative and to serve as a musician was a great privilege.

The following Monday morning I presented myself to the District office for the exam doctor, he was also thee officer Captain that was appointing directing all of us soldiers to different branches of the Military Service. that morning with me were also all of my friends from the Paese Caselle. some were destined in Cavalleria some in Artilleria some in fanteria. most of my friend fromCaselle were destined in the 64 regiment Fanteria located in Firenze.

But that cold Monday morning after the medical officer gave me a good goin over, he shouted loud abile (able) al 64 Regiment of Fanteria. I was expecting to hear Abile al servizio del 6th Regiment of RR ingeneers. I was stunned disappointed and crying. I was hurt. to make thing worst I had told some of my friend that I was going to be assigned to the RR Engineer 6th regiment stationed in Torino. When my friend heard that I was going in the Infantry regiment some of my friend made fun of me that hurt even more – it was a terrible day for me-

After some thinking one inspiration came to me, to go and see the Maestro that madder me the promise to go in the RR Engineer regiment, but we could not. At the quarters at the main door there was a guard stationed. No one of us could leave the quarter till 4 P.M. I knew in order for me to be able to see the maestro I had to be at the 6th Regiment headquarter not later than 4 P.M. so it was necessary for me to leave the headquarter before 4 P.M.. The military headquarter was about 15 minutes walk from the location of the 6th regiment of the RR Engineers, so I decided to take a chance, start running as fast as I could past the door guard so he could not catch me and stop me, keep on going. I reached the RR engineer headquarter just at the right time, the soldiers were just returning from the usual everyday maneuvering. The RR Engineer band playing, the Maestro leading and the soldiers entering the headquarter. I also entered the headquarter with the soldiers and as soon I saw the Maestro was free I went to him and told him of what happened to me that day at the induction headquarter. Told him that I was inducted in the 64th Regiment infantry, stationed in Florence Tuscany. The maestro noticed I was very much excited, told me be calm, wait for me right here I will come back after a while. in fact he did and told me to run right back to the induction headquarter where I came from and wait for somebody to call you. I did exactly as the maestro told me, run right back to my..... There was already a corporal from the office of the medical officer that was looking for me calling my name Sartore, Sartore. I presented myself – Here I am. – the corporal sayd to me the medical officer want to talk to you and he lead me to the office of the officer. The officer say to me – Soldier Sartore you will be assigned to the 6th regiment RR Engineer Rome and not to the Regiment 64th Infantry, Florence. I was elated very happy to hear this news. My whole situation changed. This was the beginning of my military life. The maestro also told me they are going to send you to a RR Engineer company in Rome, but you play dumb, do not say anything, do as you are told. So it happened they gave me a RR ticket for Rome and I followed instruction, went all the way to Rome at the RR Engineer headquarter called Fort Momentana. I sayd before on account of a quarantine due to the fact that the City of Caselle was considered an infected area we went into thee Military Service about 40 day later than most of the other recruits, so they had 40 days of basic training and some had the basic training almost finished so when I came into the service had very little basic training. At Rome I reached the Company at Fort Momentana late. there was lots activity there, lots of soldiers of the 6th regiment RR engineers. one corporal prepared a bunk for me to sleep the first night. In the morning I was presented to a lieutenant on horseback that he was asking me several questions as follows I understand you are from the City of Torino Answer: Yes – You are a musician are you? – Answer: yes – Who send you here in Rome? The musical Band of the RR Engineers is stationed in Torino, you should be in Torino, not Rome. At this point I remembered the maestro's instructions to play dumb and I did just that, played dumb. This lieutenant ordered a corporal to make preparation to send me back to Torino, but this lieutenant wanted to make sure that I was really a musician, wanted me with the trumpet to play something for him I asked him what he wanted me to play for him, he sayd play me the Vedova Allegra (The operetta happy widow). This lieutenant was completely ignorant of musical instrument. Vedova Allegra can be played with a cornet of 7 note, a bugler's trumpet has only 4 notes to play. Anyway I did play a couple of military signals to prove to the lieutenant that I could play music with a cornet. At this point the lieutenant asked a corporal to give me money (10 lire) for the ride, RR trip to go back to Torino. So I went to the main RR station of Rome, bought the ticket. It was still early in the morning so I say to myself I came to Rome and I have yet to see the city of Rome. So I asked at the information window the time the train was leaving that day for Torino and I wasld told one train leaves at 10 A.M., another leaves Rome for Torino at 6 P.M. So I figured I will go around and see the City of Rome for a few hours then take the 6 P.M. train for Torino. So I went around Rome not too far from the RR station. Noon time went in a restaurant and ate a lunch all by myself and returned to the RR station in plenty time for the 6 P.M. train that supposed to leave the Central Rome Station for Torino. and asked of those red cap officer where was the line for me to board the 6 o'clock train for Torino…on the right side of where I was standing was a number of empty coaches. The station officer pointed to me those coaches so I went right in one of them and waited and waited. It was past 6 P.M. I got off the train and asked another red cap officer of the station when the 6 P.M. train leaves for Torino. I was told the train that just left. I then realize that the coaches that I went on were not part of the train that went to Torino. I was left there. So I was really in trouble. not much money in my pocket. What to do? So I decided to go back to the RR Engineer headquarter Via Momentana and spend the night there. So I did just that, the soldiers in seeing me come back were asking me question why I returned back to the Fort Momentana. I had to explain what happened to me that day – it was into evening then. One of the corporal gave me some bread to eat then he prepared for me a place to sleep for the night. The next morning I had to face again the same lieutenant officer. He asked me why the reason I did not leave for Torino, but first asked me if I had the 10 lire bill that he gave me to buy pay for the RR trip fare to go to Torino, and I answered I do not have the 10 lire, but I still have the ticket that I purchased the day before. When I sayd that the lieutenant was much more relieved. He then asked a corporal to accompany me all the way to the Central Station, to put me on the train leaving for Torino and to make sure I was leaving Rome and go straight to Torino. So I was on my way to Torino. I arrived late that evening and instead going to present myself to the Headquarter of RR engineer I went straight back to my home with my brother Pietro where I was living before going into the army and sleep there. The next morning I presented myself to the maestro. He asked me you just arrive now from Rome? I sayd no, I did arrived late last night. I thought better for me to go home for the night, return this morning in the headquarter to see you and ask for instruction of what to do next. The maestro scolded me he sayd don't you know that you are now a soldier and you should act like one. Up to that time I was still dressed in my civilian clothes. From this day was the start of my military life with the 6th Regiment of RR Engineers Musical band. So by coming in late and dilly dally around I came into the army without hardly doing any basic training and started rehersing and playing my trumpet in the RR engineer band for the following 28 months. It was a good life maybe the best time of my life was spend there. In the afternoon after service I used to go almost every evening to eat supper at my sisters house. Then after supper I used to return to the headquarter and sleep with the other soldiers of the musical band. On weekends and Sunday often I used to take the train and go to Caselle and spend the Sunday to visit my brother, sometime getting together with the musicians of the Caselle musical band, sometime to see my sister Giulia in the evening I used to return to the RR engineers headquarter and for another week same thing all over again. It was not a bad life.After about one year of this life, in the year 1911 Italy declared war on the Arab Country of Libya. It was called the Libyan war, Italy fought and conquered Tripoli, Bengasi, Cirenaica andTripolitania. The regiment of the 64th infantry was one of the first troop to be sent there to fight in the battle against the Arab and Turk soldier. These were my friend from the town of Caselle where I was born, these were brave soldiers that I almost was myself one of them. Fact happen almost all of them did not return home and die in the service of their country. The city of Caselle wanted to remember these brave soldiers, these heros, so the city in memory of these heros planted two rows of trees one on each side of a road on each one of the trees there is a bronze plaque attached to the tree on it there is the name of one of the hero that die in the Libyan war. Name such as Giardino Giuseppe, caduto (fallen) date etc etc in the service of his country. the road was named Via dei martiri (Road of the Martyrs). Today this road with all those tall trees with the bronze plate on each one of them is still there a testimonial of what happened during the Libyan war. When I went to Caselle the first time in the year 1969 I saw these bronze plaques and reminded myself that I too could have been one of them dead soldiers. I thank God that give the inspiration after I was inducted in the 64 regiment 64th infantry. The maestro saved my life by helping me to be part of the RR engineer band and spared my life. During the years 1911-1912 the RR engineer band was doing service by going to the RR station picking up soldiers returning home from the Libyan war, or accompany other soldiers going to fight the Libyan war. Most of our time was spend this way, and I thank the good Lord I was lucky not to be send to fight in that war. The end of this war came around the end of the year 1912. In February 1913 I was sent home to again live a civilian life and returned to work at the Industrie Metallurgiche; but my plan was to emigrate and to come to America to provide better opportunity for myself – my future life, but it took money to make a trip to America, lots of money. So my brother Giuseppe loaned me some 440 lire enough to pay for one trip in 3rd class steerage for one person to make the trip from LeHavre French port to NewYork, on the French boat La France, a big boat that even at that time was crossing the North Sea in eight days leaving Le Havre port on one Saturday and reaching New York Ellis Hyland the following Saturday. So I got busy went to Caselle where I was born asked the communal authority for permission to emigrate to North America, asked them to make me the passport and all the necessary paper required for such a trip, which they did.

This trip consisted of leaving Torino one afternoon on a train, travel on the train the rest of the day and all night reaching the port of LeHavre the following day in order to board the boat that leaved LeHavre for New York. For me that trip on the boat was a terrible trip. the sea was most of the time very bad I was vomiting all the time could not hold anything in my stomac. I was very sick so sick that I swore if I make this trip to the other side to New York I will never never go on another boat again. Well thank God we finally made it to Ellis Island. On this trip I forgot to mention that I had a friend of mine from Torino coming with me to New York and finally coming to live in Pittsburgh Pa – he had a cousin living in Pgh – he was coming to reach his cousin. I had no one personal relative, no friend waiting for me in Pittsburgh. I was depending on my friends cousin to help me find a place for myself, We finally got off the boat and all emigrants were driven in a building – walking with rail on each side of us like cattle in a long line. Finally I was facing a desk where an emigration officer was sitting and asking questions to me such as your name etc for what reason you are coming to America, what is your profession, speaking in a very bad Italian, sayd have you ever been incarcerated and other question that I have now forgotten. Finally he sayd go ahead. I felt very good knowing I had passed the test probably knowing I had a trade. I was a mechanic. I believed did help me a lot. Most of us emigrant from Italy were plain laborers, not many had a profession. May 31, 1913 I landed in New York Ellis Island. toward the evening of the same day together with many hundred emigrant of many different country I was transported with a boat to the B&O station. Each one of us it was given a brown bag containing some food, one loaf of stale bread one pce of baloney one small apple. This was all the food to sustained me until we reached Pittsburgh. The train left N. Y. for Pittsburg toward the evening same day. We traveled all night, the next day it was Sunday morning. toward before noon we reached Pgh B&) station near Smithfield St. bridge. My friends cousin Sebastiano Zorniotti was waiting for us at the station. The day was June 1st 1913---it was terrible hot that day. I still remember how appreciative I was when a bottle of cold beer was offered to us. this cousin of my friend took us to a boarding house where he was living and we were received cordially with the other boarders – and the house lady. We soon found out that in 1913 in Pittsburg was a depression time and very hard to find a job of any kind, even a manual kind digging ditch or whatever it was offered to me, to make thing more difficult we did not understand a word of Inglish-a job was offered to us in dormont or brookline to load trucks with a shovel all day lifting dirt from the ground to the truck. In the evening I had blisters on my hand that hurt my hand terrible, my back could not take that kind of work. Next day we were unable to show for work with all my blistered hand and my aching back. The pay for this kind of work was two dollars per day but I could not continue this kind of work. I was not used to this kind of work. In those days the cost of room and board was not high 30 dollars per month was the price we used to pay for having the privileges of sleeping in one bed, usually a folding cot, and two meals a day, lunchmeal we had to provide ourselves. the lady of the house was even doing the washing of some of our shirts and underwear for the price of 30 dollars per month. This pick and shovel job was called digging ditch with pick and shovel but this kind of a job was not for me. I was worried because when end of month came I had no money to pay my room and board, but the house lady was compassionate, a very good person, she told me do not worry you will pay me when you find a job. My second attempt to get a job. A fellow which we became good friend name Noe (Noah) offered to take me with him to work in a coal mine, somewhere in Bruceton Pa. this friend did help me to get the job in the coal mine with him and took me to buy the pick and shovel, cap, electric light, battery etc, all the equipment necessary to work with him as his partner, his buddies as they used to call each other at that time. The following morning the mine forman took us inside of the mine. we went through a big hole inside of a hill with our tools, rubber boots, cap and light, forman first, my friend second, and I the last one, kept on walking for ½ hour or more, the passage was low and narrow, often times my lamp was hitting some of the rocks projecting from the roof. I had a very hard time. They were used to walking curved down. For me was terrible hard, because they were walking rather fast. Finally the mine boss stopped and pointed out to us here, this is your place of work – note we were in a hole in the ground we were working approximately 8 or ten inches of water we were supposed to bend down and with the pick dig the coal out of the rock, the slab or vein of coal was about 3 feet thick, load coal on a small car and push the car when loaded on a small track for the main train to pick it up and bring the car outside of the mine. When I saw that I felt almost like crying. I told Noe, my partner, Noe I can't do this kind of work; but he sayd to me this post is only for a while, only for the beginning, later on we will be given a better post to work, a post with no water in the floor. well the same day I decided to return back to pittsburgh to live in the boarding house where my friend Zorniotti used to live and waited for a better opportunity. One day a job from an ice cream factory was offered to my friend Zorniotti, this job consisted of washing containers called freezers, were galvanized can container for icecream of 1-2-3-4-5-gallon each that 3 or 4 horses drawn wagon were used to deliver icecream to grocery stores throughout the city of Pgh. *End of notes.*

Nephew's Quest Ends
In Thurber Cemetery

Fort Worth Star Telegram   **John McConal's**
22 February 1993   **Texas**

Thurber – Forgive Gino Sartore if he seemed excited as he drank coffee in the New York Hill Restaurant. After all, he was about to see for the first time the grave of the first member of the Sartore family to be buried in this country.

The grave is that of his uncle, Giovanni Sartore, who came to this country in the late 1800s to work in the Thurber coal mines.

The mines, most of which closed in 1921 because of a massive strike, attracted thousands of immigrants. Many had left behind families they would never see again except in fading photographs.

"My father had two wishes before he died," said Gino Sartore, who had come here from Pittsburgh. "He wanted to see the grave of his brother and he wanted to see what the country around here looked like." He stirred his coffee.

"Unfortunately, he died before that happened." Sartore said.

The fact that any of the Sartore family would be able to see the grave is due in large part to chance and in another part to the meticulous work of the Thurber Cemetery Association in restoring the cemetery during the last year.

"There were over 1,000 people buried up there," said Leo Bielinski, who has helped in that effort. "But so far we have only identified 300 of the graves." *The grave of Sartore's uncle is one of those 300.*

Sartore told the story in this once thriving town, which is 60 miles west of Fort Worth on Interstate 20.

His uncle was the oldest in a family of four boys and three girls.

"My father (Lorenzo) was only 7 when he (Giovanni) came to America. But as far as we can tell, he worked in the coal mines near Pittsburgh before coming here in about 1897," Sartore said. Apparently, soon after his arrival he joined the company band, called the Hunter's Band. He played the trombone. Bielinski, who has done tons of research on the area, showed a copy of a picture of Giovanni in his band uniform. He is dressed in a fancy uniform and has a lock of dark hair falling across his forehead. Sartore said he heard his father talk about his uncle for most of his life. So when Sartore was attending a Dallas convention about 14 years ago, he rented a car and drove here for the first time. He tried unsuccessfully to find his uncle's grave.

"The cemetery was so overgrown," he said. But he told Les Mullins of Hereford about his efforts. One day Mullins stopped and made a two-hour unsuccessful search of the cemetery. He left his card at the nearby Mingus City Hall. Somebody gave it to Bielinski.

"My hair stood up on my neck," Bielinski said. "We had just dug up a broken tombstone and were putting it back together. It apparently belonged to Gino's uncle."

After confirmation, Sartore returned last week to look at his uncle's marker.

We drove past foothills clotted with mesquite and the site of some old coal mines where Giovanni could have worked.

We went to the Thurber Cemetery on top of a mesa and stopped at the Sartore marker which was engraved in Italian. Sartore translated the words: "Born June 20, 1875; died March 29, 1901," he said. "And on the top that is 'Star of Italy.' We think that must have been some lodge."

Lettering on the bottom is broken. But Sartore knelt, felt it and finally said. "I've got it. It's 'Pray for his soul.' "

He stood up. Tony Sico, his associate, took his photograph. Sartore, 72, is lanky. The wind caught his hair, dashing it onto his forehead. It looked just like that falling into his uncle's face with one difference. Gino's hair is white.

BEER, BOOZE, BOOTLEGGING
AND BOCCI BALL
IN THURBER-MINGUS

bootlegger – an allusion to concealing whisky on the leg of a high boot; one who sells illicit alcoholic beverages.

*W*hen Thurber coal production was cut back in 1921, union miners had to vacate Thurber houses and relocate. Many went to coal mines in Illinois.

In 1922 the RR car repair yard, located 1-1/2 miles north of Thurber, was permanently shut down when its fifty workers went on strike in support of the miners. In 1926 the last two mines closed. Then came the Depression. In 1932 the Thurber Brick Plant shut down, and in 1933 Texas Pacific Oil Company moved its headquarters to Fort Worth. With the exception of eight structures, all buildings and houses in Thurber were torn down or moved away, and Thurber became a ghost town. But the Thurber-Mingus locale did not feel the full impact of these events until after repeal of Prohibition in 1933 because from 1920 to 1933 this area was the "Bootleg Capitol of Texas". And bootlegging was economically beneficial not only to the bootlegger but to the entire community, in spite of the stigma.

When Thurber began its decline in 1921, the ex-miners who lived in nearby Thurber Junction were trapped. They had their dream, a piece of America, a mortgaged home which could not be sold; therefore, they could not move to other locations to seek work. Fortunately, the Volstead Act of 1919, which banned alcoholic beverages, became the salvation of those caught in this situation. And bootlegging became a means of providing for their families.

With the nearby 1917 Ranger Oil Boom spreading to Hogtown, Eastland, Breckenridge, Caddo etc., the oil field workers were thirsty customers of the Mingus bootleggers. Several families made small fortunes from bootlegging and were able to live off their earnings until WWII. At the height of the Great Depression several ex-bootleggers bought new cars!

When historians think of depressed areas, most think of Appalachia. But the Thurber/Mingus area in the mid-1930s was probably worse off than Appalachia because many families in Thurber/Mingus existed on $24 a month, sometimes less than that when WPA funds were short. A meal might depend on hunting or fishing skills. Squirrels, rabbits, possum, field larks, ducks and doves. At night, using dogs and carbide lamps, boys hunted for pelts: coon, possum, fox and skunk.

As a youngster, the writer lived on "Bootleg Alley," the heart of the bootlegging industry. Even sixty years after the bootlegging days, many bootlegger descendants are reluctant to have their names associated with that era; therefore, in the accompanying article, most names are disguised.

In 1928 a stranger came into Mingus and stopped at Peggy Lynn's garage and asked, "Where can I get some beer?" Peggy pointed to the Baptist Church. "See that Church?" "Yes." "See that building with the flag?" "Yes." "Well, that's the Baptist Church and the Post Office. You can get a beer anyplace but those two buildings."

When the coal mines closed in 1921, Thurber began a decline from a population of 6,000 to a Ghost Town. A brick smokestack, three brick buildings and three houses, halfway between Fort Worth and Abilene, on I-20, mark the remains of this once vibrant city. The adjoining town of Mingus, which was economically dependent on Thurber, also diminished in population from about 1800 to less than 300 people today. In spite of the dwindled population, this area has one unique feature: it has never been "dry." Mingus has long been known as the only "wet" place for miles around and at one time it could count one saloon for every eighteen residents. Today, about half the citizens are in some way associated with alcoholic beverages.

Thurber-Mingus' "wetness" can be attributed to its originally foreign-born populace which came to this locale around the turn of the century for work in the mines. Drinking was an essential part of everyday life for these Eastern European immigrants: religion, celebrations, wine or beer with meals and something to "cut" the coal dust. Gino Solignanni recalled one Italian custom for holidays wherein several men would get together and walk from house to house of friends, serenade the family, wish the family well and then sample the premise's refreshments. Seven homes seemed to be the most the happy group could visit on an outing.

Bocci ball is a colorful Italian game which is still played in Mingus. Beer and bocci ball go hand in hand because the losers buy the beer. With four men on each side, the object is to get each ball closest to the baa-ling, a small target ball. The game can be played on virtually any open ground. When beer was legal, the miners would load a wagon with a barrel of beer and a head of cheese.

They would play down a dirt road and about mid-afternoon the direction of play would be reversed back toward Thurber. The winner of each game (twelve points) got beer and cheese. At the end of the day, the number of games won by each side was about even.

During Prohibition the bocci players had to take to the woods so they could play bocci and drink homebrew without being raided. One bocci court was hidden away on County Commissioner Bob Loflin's wooded property. The "Law" would not dare raid the popular Commissioner's private domain.

During the Depression of the '30s, an inexpensive evening would be to watch the bocci players at a lighted court on the side of Pete Taramino's saloon and drink ten-cent beer or three for a quarter. Brands included Red Fox, Black Dallas, Harry Mitchell, Fox DeLuxe, ABC, Old Style Lager, Southern Select, Grand Prize, Muehlbach. Another lighted court was on the side of Meneghetti's Saloon.

Drinking and saloons were a part of the history of Thurber and the associated labor movement. The first saloon was near Mine Shaft Number 1. When Thurber began to grow, the Texas and Pacific Coal Company established the "Snake" Saloon in downtown Thurber and a second saloon, "The Lizard", on Polander Hill. When Erath County went "dry" in 1904, a new "Snake" saloon was built just inside the Palo Pinto County line. In 1913 the company bought 11,737 barrels and 777 casks of beer at a cost of $89,438.31. Under the supervision of Mr. Gustaves, the company provided a handy service to beer lovers: free delivery with purchase of a barrel of beer.

The miners sometimes took beer or wine to work in miner's pails. The food was kept in the top of the container and the drink in the bottom of the pail. After work there might be a stop at the saloon to refill the pail for the evening meal.

With such high beer consumption, a seemingly profitable opportunity was the establishment of the Mingus Brewery around 1908 at Mingus Little Lake. But the brewery never prospered and was torn down a few years later. It is not known whether this small brewery could compete against big city breweries or whether the coal company would buy the beer.

One of the early settlers of an area between Thurber and Mingus was a man named Grant who had a saloon just outside the coal company property. This place was referred to as Grant's Town or Grant Town, as it is known locally. About 1892 Grant sold his saloon to Bruce and Stewart and the place became a hotbed of union activity because union organizers were not permitted on company land. Colonel Hunter, President of T & P, closed the road which ran by the saloon and the owners took Hunter to court for closing a public road. But the court ruled in favor of Hunter. Stewart then distributed circulars in Thurber advertising free beer:

...Boys drink with us; we are among you; we are one of you... We will give free beer to the public from 12 o'clock noon. until 9 o'clock at night, on next Saturday, June 2nd, 1894. Saloon just outside of the wire (the fence around Thurber).

Of course, while the miners were guzzling free beer, the union organizers worked on them. It was a long, bitter battle but the Union was finally granted a charter on October 8, 1903.

After the mines closed and prohibition was in full force, bootlegging became a matter of survival for many. Many of the immigrants now had large families and a return to the Old Country was unthinkable. As one ex-bootlegger put it, "Hell, nobody thought of it bein' agin' the law. It was a way of makin' a livin'." For the miners who lived in company-owned houses in Thurber, they had to move on when the city began to fold. For those who owned their own homes in Mingus and could not get a job with the oncoming oil industry, the choice was more difficult. With the Ranger oil boom fifteen miles to the west, bootlegging became very profitable.

But even before the Volstead Act of 1919, which established prohibition, the Italians made wine for home use and for use as altar wine in the Catholic Church at Thurber. This church, built in 1892, was moved to Mingus in 1936 and then back to Thurber in 1993. It is still structurally sound and beautiful in its simplicity.

Carloads of grapes would be shipped in from California and the Italian school kids with grapes in their lunch bags had many friends. The Italians used the leftover grape skins from wine to produce a "grappo" (grape) whisky which was about 170 proof. To the grape skins, sugar and water were added to produce drinkable ethyl alcohol. With prohibition, the genuine "grappo" whisky was made from raisins which could be bought in wooden crates or in sacks from Angelo Reck's store or other grocers. However, some whisky was made from anything which fermented: peach skins and stones, apples and pears, all of which grew locally. The Mingus "grappo" whisky differed from other bootleg whisky in that most "other" whisky was made from grain and mash.

Mingus was also known as Thurber Junction for the rail spur to Thurber from the main line at Mingus. But in the '20s, there was a third name: "Grappo Junction."

The Italians had a saying: "Fresh bread and old wine." The wine was available. The bread came from outdoor brick ovens and was baked once or twice a week, about twelve loaves at a time. This delicious white bread with a thick, hard crust was in such demand that some families such as the Biondini and Meneghetti had regular customers to whom they delivered bread. Leftover dough was used to make "cornutti," a small, hard-crusted roll. Mrs. Marine served this bread as late as 1950 with her spaghetti and "wop" salad in her restaurant/saloon.

About two hundred families engaged in making and selling beer and whisky during Prohibition. For most families it was a necessity. Others made small fortunes and drove big cars. It has been estimated the bootlegging industry grossed about a million dollars a year for all involved. After the repeal of Prohibition and during the hard times of the Depression, until WWII, ex-bootleggers were able to live off their earnings. There was none of the gangsterism or organized crime which was prevalent in the larger cities during this era. It was a family type operation.

The big bootleggers had some business as a front. One feed store had three Mexicans working full time making "grappo". A garage mechanic would back his Model T pickup into the feed store. Bottles of whisky would go on the bottom, sacks of feed on top. This mechanic's services were in demand, for he got calls at all hours of the night and day to go "fix" broken-down cars. Another trick was to put bottles of whisky in sacks of feed. It did not matter if there were no chickens or cows to feed. The unused feed would be exchanged for another sack of "feed", time and again.

Under-house basements are not common in Texas but several bootleggers had basements to conceal their liquor. The trapdoor was hidden by a rug or a bed or merchandise. At least three stores and several homes were known to have this arrangement.

The largest dealer was strictly a wholesaler with a dry goods store as a front. He had several people supplying him. He concealed his wealth very well by banking long distance with a St. Louis bank.

One bootlegger had four daughters, each of whom made a weekly trip with a large suitcase to Fort Worth. A man named Marconi dressed as a priest and made frequent excursions to Dallas carrying a large black suitcase. A brakeman on a "local" train with a daily run between Mingus and Ranger would buy a gallon of 170 proof "grappo" and cut it with water to make two gallons or eight quarts. He stashed this in his "working bag" and doubled his money in the boomtown of Ranger. His weekly profit was about $100.

One man was known for his "fancy" booze, such as peach brandy. He sold all he made to the Thurber Club, a private club for the executives and staff of the reorganized Texas and Pacific Coal and Oil Company. Bars were not legal, even in a private club. But after each dance set, members would "beeline" to individual lockers for a "nip." This bootlegger lived in Mingus but had his still on a farm south of Thurber. No one ever visited his farm because access was through four gates, each with a large padlock. Folks evidently saw no wrong in bootlegging, or did not know this man bootlegged, for he was later elected to a county office.

For those with a more "exotic" taste, ersatz rye whisky was available from a dealer who held a "patent" on the process. The "patent" was obtained from a northerner and was nothing more than a few secret ingredients added to the grappo. It is known that root beer syrup was one of the additives. The man with the rye secret refused to share it with Old Man Vecera. This galled Vecera who then began mixing up different flavored whiskies by simply adding juice, extract or flavoring to the grappo. Strawberry grappo was a specialty but the best seller was a banana grappo, and Vecera got revenge by never sharing the banana recipe with anyone.

The Mingus bootleggers were clever in their use of an oval-shaped, copper, clothes boiling pot as the still. First, it could be broken down completely with no resemblance to a still. Secondly, all households, bootlegger or non-bootlegger, used a clothes boiling pot. Thirdly, with a fire going under the pot, was someone boiling clothes or making illicit hootch?

In the Mingus still, copper tubing ran from the lid of the pot into coils (the worm) inside a wooden barrel which contained ice or water. The tubing then exited out a cork stopper in the side of the barrel. A jug at the end of the tubing caught the drips of ethyl alcohol. The lid and the tubing hole in the lid were sealed with a paste made of flour and water. A mesquite fire sometimes heated the pot. But a better set-up was a double burner kerosene stove where the heat could be controlled. The distilled whisky came off clear. But sugar was browned in a skillet and added to give the desired amber color. One old-timer pointed out the advantages of using a copper still: "Nobody in Mingus or Grant Town ever sold any bad whisky. The copper don't mix with the whisky. Hell, I've heard of people around Glen Rose being poisoned because someone used a barrel or a tin tub for a still. You don't get a spoiled taste when you use copper."

Most whisky makers used ice with the Mingus Still because the ice "drawed the whisky out." "The best ice in the world," made from distilled water, was conveniently available at the Thurber Ice Plant for seventy-five cents a 300-pound block. The Thurber Power Plant was steam-driven. Distilled water, condensed from steam, was fed into the ice vats. There were advantages in using distilled water in making ice; no mineral residue left in the vats and no clogged pipes.

I.P. Rainwater (yes) was a well-liked iceman in Mingus. Tony Aria also delivered ice, and later, Bill Peretti. There were a few other icemen. The iceman who delivered to the bootlegger was a man who saw nothing and "kept his mouth shut." F.T. and O.R. had several batches of grappo to run off and they sent their iceman after several blocks of ice. Now, this was a suspiciously large amount of ice to Mr. Lee, who was in charge of the ice plant and he refused to sell the ice. "I know what it's for. It's for the bootleggers. And bootlegging is against the law." The iceman went to W.K. Gordon, General Manager of all Thurber operations, and explained his problem. W.K. called Lee. "Mr. Lee, please understand that all ice we make is for sale to anybody, and it's none of our business what it's used for."

One prominent rancher loved grappo but would pass out "cold" sometimes and not remember a thing for a day or two. He feared that he might be mistaken for dead and be buried alive. While he was still living, he had a telephone line strung to the family burial plot in Davidson Cemetery. His Will stipulated that a telephone be placed in his hand, inside his coffin, and if he did not call out within three days, he was sure to be dead and not just passed out.

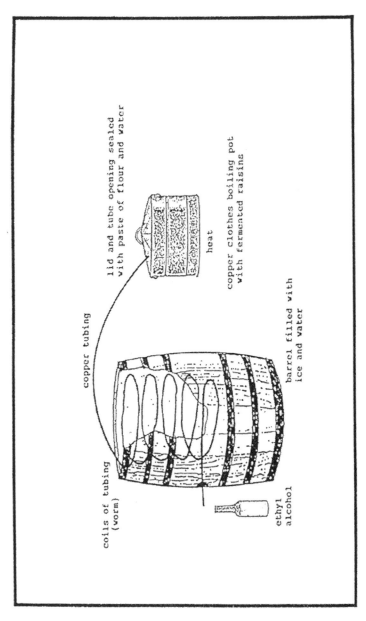

GRAPPO STILL USED IN THURBER-MINGUS

In addition to grappo whisky, bootleg beer was made. This homebrew beer was called "chalk beer" for the white, chalk-like sediment at the bottom of the bottle. Bottles, caps, a capper, rubber tubing, a crock, water, malt, yeast and sugar were the essentials. Cans of malt, "Bulldog" or "Blue Ribbon" brand, as well as bottle caps, could be bought at any grocery store. Good water was evidently the key to good homebrew. Most of the well water was "hard" water which necessitated that cisterns and barrels catch rain water. Some homes had wells which caught seep water from an adjoining pond and some families went to Thurber to get barrels and jugs of water. During dry weather, Tony Aria's water truck would refill a cistern or well with water from the Mingus Little Lake. The water situation prompted a humorous, often-quoted saying: "Let's make some homebrew. I can get ten gallons of good creek water."

If the homebrew was bottled too soon, or if the stored homebrew got hot, there might be a mess from exploding bottles. One Italian bootlegger lost his left eye from an exploding bottle.

While the majority of bootleggers were Italians, all nationalities were participants. Sherman Fehls, of Graham, Texas recalled that in the '20s his group would make a weekly beer run from Eastland to Grant Town. A black lady, known as "Nigger Jenny," made good homebrew. While "Nigger Jenny" cooked up a batch of fried chicken, each man enjoyed two or three bottles of beer. Then a bottle or two with the delicious fried chicken. Sometimes there were four men in Sherman's group, sometimes five. But the total bill for the chicken and beer for the whole group was always the same: "Fiv'dollah be too much?" "Nigger Jenny" Moore was killed in the early '30s by a shotgun blast from a neighbor in an argument over a property line. The shotgun wielder got a four-year suspended sentence. That was justice of the times: a suspended sentence for a killing, but two years "straight" in the pen for bootlegging.

Few chances were taken when selling illegal beverages. Before a bottle was sold to a new customer, a known customer would have to accompany and vouch for the new customer during the initial purchase. If the buyer was a good customer or a friend of the dealer, he was allowed to "visit" on the back porch or under a secluded shade tree and drink his whisky or beer without having to transport it. Drinking whetted the appetite which made the "Dutch Lunch" very popular around Mingus because this lunch required no elaborate preparation, no cooking, few dishes and little clean-up in the event of a hasty departure. Slices of homemade salami, Genoa salami, ham, two kinds of cheese, sliced onion, Italian peppers and Italian bread with a bottle of homebrew made a satisfying meal.

With bootlegging, came raids by the "Law." But the bootleggers always seemed to be forewarned and not too many dealers were caught with the "goods." Gabe Mayo, of Gordon, Texas, was a friendly, local constable who liked his booze and who tipped off the bootleggers. There were three possible violations under the Volstead Act: manufacturing, possessing or the selling of intoxicating beverages. But there were several factors working in the bootlegger's favor. In 1925 there were about 40,000 bootleggers in Texas and only forty agents to cover all of Texas and Oklahoma. The Federal Agents were often assisted by friendly, local law enforcement officials. Ma Ferguson, Governor of Texas, was issuing clemency proclamations, right and left. And Ma was easy on bootlegging, a victimless crime. Many times the person seeking clemency was represented by Jim Ferguson, Ma Ferguson's husband, who had been previously impeached as Governor. As of August 30, 1926, Ma had issued 2,323 conditional pardons, paroles and furloughs. The reasons for clemency would often be "sickness in family...death in family...request of Mayor...petition of citizens" etc. Several Mingus bootleggers served short stints in jail.

The Dry Agents were ruthless, crude and destructive. Whisky was found at a Polander's house near New No. 1 Mine in 1924 or

1925. The Pole panicked and ran. The agent shot him. Pinky Wylie of Thurber could not recall the Pole's name but remembered the agent was one-armed. This killing was unnecessary and increased the animosity toward Prohibition Agents.

During raids, vegetable and flower gardens would be trampled. Once, an acre of corn was flattened. Gates for livestock and chickens would be left open. Clothes and boxes from closets scattered about. Bricks and rocks from under house siding strewn everywhere. The wreckage was left to the family to clean up. When a raid was on, the bootlegger's children often would be sent to neighboring homes so as not to divulge the hiding places.

When raids were conducted the bootleggers tried to hide out so they would not be arrested or served a summons. Sometimes a traveling judge came with the dry agents. If the raid were successful, court might be held the same day in Dan Raffael's grocery store in Grant Town. Or, the bootlegger was tried later in county court.

Booze was discovered at one home but the bootlegger hid under the house. All day long the agent would periodically shout for the whole neighborhood to hear: "Come out, Sam. We know you're under there."

Mrs. Kraschmier usually fled to Mrs. Daskevich's secluded home about a quarter-mile away. Access was along a narrow, wooded path and across a long, foot-wide, creaky bridge. One day Mrs. Kraschmier, a widow in her sixties, failed to get the word and was caught making homebrew in her kitchen. She was sentenced to a year and a half. But the sentence was suspended when it was learned she was the sole support of a deaf son.

Two or three dry agents, accompanied by the legendary lawman, Si Bradford, the County Sheriff and Constable Gabe Mayo usually conducted the raids. Si helped capture the bandits in the famous 1927 Santa Claus bank robbery of Cisco, Texas. Si killed several men in the line of duty. Si always carried a pointed, metal rod on raids with which he tapped and probed. When he tapped hollow on a false panel of a chimney, the bootlegger took off running. "Stop, or I'll kill you dead!" bellowed Si. The bootlegger stopped because he knew Si would.

One bootlegger had two German shepherd pups which were killed by a bulldog. He buried the dogs in the woods behind his home. Si's metal probe tapped a suspicious sound. "Come on, boys. I've found it." But Si was disappointed to find two badly-decomposed dogs.

A fisherman used a bootlegger's pond to suspend his minnows by a pole in deeper water to keep the minnows fresh. When Si Bradford failed to reset the pole after checking it for whiskey, the minnows died and Si had to make restitution to the irate fisherman.

As a sixteen-year-old, Andrew Marine innocently went to a friend's home when agents were raiding the friend's home. The agent jumped Andrew and threatened to "run him in" unless he told where the stuff was hidden. Repeatedly, Andrew said, "I don't live here. I'm only sixteen." The agent said, "You're a smart SOB!" and whacked Andrew on the jaw, knocking him into a Victrola and smashing it. Andrew got up and started for the agent who put his hand on his gun. Andrew yelled, "You're the smart SOB. Run me in and hear what I tell the judge!" The agent still thought Andrew would "crack" and did "run him in" for the hearings. Four others were tried before Andrew. When the judge beckoned Andrew forward, the agent said, "That's all, Your Honor," and quickly whisked Andrew out the door and released him.

At two A.M. one morning during a cold rain, there was a knocking at a bootlegger's door. A man was in a raincoat, covered with and smelling of oil and wore muddy, knee length, laced boots, which were popular at this time. "Say, Jim, I'm tool pusher on a well we just brought in at Ex-Ray (south of Thurber). It's a miserable night and my men told me to get two quarts from you so we could warm up and celebrate the new well." And he mentioned the names of a few men Jim knew. Jim asked a few questions and knew better but sold the caller two quarts. The man was a dry agent.

A twenty-year-old was arrested for bootlegging and got two years. A lawyer from Mineral Wells was a frequent visitor to Mingus. The family shelled out $1,600 and the lawyer paid off someone to get the young man released. He served only two days of the sentence.

Art's close friend, "Slim," was sent to Huntsville on a two-year term. After serving several months, Slim suddenly died. The body was shipped home to Strawn Merchandise Company for burial with closed coffin instructions. The undertaker knew Art and said "Art, I know you and Slim were real close. I'm not supposed to do this, but there's something odd about the body. See what you think." According to Art, the face was dark purple. There was an incision from the breast bone to the navel. The incision was crudely stitched up with straw sticking out between the stitches. Prison officials would not admit anything. Slim's widow contacted one of Slim's cell-mates, a man from Stephenville. He wrote, "I cannot tell you anything, now. In a year's time, I'll be out; then I can talk." It seems that Slim and two other inmates were sold poisonous wood alcohol whisky by a guard. Two inmates were blinded; Slim died. All the organs were removed to prevent an autopsy and to prevent a possible scandal. It was a strange twist that after making many gallons of good, pure "grappo" whisky, Slim should perish by bad whisky.

To the people of Mingus, Andrew Marine's warning ride was comparable to Paul Revere's ride. The Feds were fed up with the bootleggers being tipped off by local law officials. One morning early, a dozen agents from Fort Worth drove into town in two big black cars. Andrew instantly recognized the strangers as agents and rode all over town and down back alleys, car horn blaring. With his head out the window he yelled, "Hide it! Hide it! Law's coming!"

Only two bootleggers were caught. A Fort Worth paper's headline the next day: "PAUL REVERE RIDES MINGUS STREETS TO WARN OF PRO-RAIDERS." The paper could not identify the mystery rider. And the whole town knew who the rider was, but no one would tell.

During the mining days, many homes had small wooden structures in back which were called "batches" where several bachelor miners bunked. When the mines closed some bootleggers converted the vacant "batches" into work areas for bootlegging. One man built a double wall and a false floor in his batch. The agents discovered the false floor, but no beer. The fermenting beer was stashed in the double wall. "Come on, Luigi. We know it's here, we can smell it. Where is it?" The agents never found it.

There was a reclusive, known only as "Frenchy," who lived in a sparse, one-room shack north of Auda's Grocery. Sometimes he did small tasks for Auda. Vic Creighton, the bread man, would toss Frenchy a loaf of bread each morning. At night he would pound continuously on the table with a spoon, for hours on end, supposedly sending messages to France. Kids would torment him by throwing rocks at his shack and once he blasted away with his shotgun. There were many stories about Frenchy. He and two brothers, all unmarried, came over from France. They dug a pond entirely by hand; pick, shovel and wheelbarrow. The water was needed for making grappo. They sold only to other bootleggers, or else, rented their still and facilities to other bootleggers. One story has Frenchy serving time in the pen; "framed" for bootlegging. Whatever happened; put Frenchy's mind off. No one ever knew Frenchy's first name. The official court documents sentencing Frenchy to jail for bootlegging list the name Frenchy Lamoureaux. The most likely scenario for his prison time is that a prominent bootlegger was caught but he was able to frame Frenchy for this violation.

One bootlegger failed to get the word on an impending raid and as the officers were coming through his front yard, he quickly threw several cases behind the front door. The dry agents never thought to look in such an obvious place.

Of eleven families who lived on "Bootlegger's Alley" in Mingus, seven bootlegged and two made liquor for their own consumption. There was considerable activity and scurrying about in this neighborhood during raiding days.

The writer, as an eight-year-old, discovered a whisky cache in a trash dump at the rear of an Italian's home. A small tub, filled with dirt and a cactus growing out of it, set flush with the ground in a buried barrel. It was found because rain had washed concealing dirt off the edges. Some bootleggers put a red cherry in each bottle of grappo. "They" say the cherry took the sting out of the grappo. After sampling and gagging, the cherry was being relished by this writer when the Old Italian appeared behind the back fence, screaming Italian curses. Needless to say, the cache was relocated.

As any visitor will attest, the people of Mingus are very cordial when they become acquainted with a person. But years of clandestine operations and raids have left a tinge of xenophobia, a suspicion of strangers, even today. In WWII, investigations for secret clearances for the Mingus servicemen were often delayed for long periods or never granted because the closemouthed Mingusites would not cooperate with OSI. This was a touchy situation because many of the servicemen's parents were born in Italy, America's enemy at this time. As one father told his Army Air Corps son about those "damn question man": "No be worry, boy, me no tell 'um damn t'ing".

Shortly after WWII an Army veteran came to Mingus to visit his wartime buddy who lived in Mingus. He walked into a saloon where a boisterous game of "shoot the moon" dominoes was in progress. "Excuse me," he addressed the group. "I'm looking for Walter Symanski." Clacking dominoes and loud talk fell dead silent. A long uneasy pause endured. Then, "Why you lookin' for him?"

When the Volstead Act was repealed in 1933, Thurber was being demolished or moved away, house by house. The Ranger oil boom had fizzled out and the Depression was on. Palo Pinto County legalized beer and wine, no whisky. Now, a bootlegger was one who bought whisky in Fort Worth and sold it in a no-whisky area. Eighteen people opened saloons or beer-to-go places. The drinking establishments were referred to by several names: saloons, beer joints, beer halls, beer places, drinking places, honky tonks, taverns, night clubs, dance halls or just the person's name.

The second floor of the Eagles Hall featured weekly dances with Pete Taramino as a no-nonsense bouncer. Drinks were not allowed but between dances and at intermissions, beer could be bought at any of the saloons scattered throughout town. Music was by Papa Sam Cunningham and his Crystal Springs Ramblers, by Milton Brown and his Musical Brownies or by the Wanderers.

During WWII there was a shortage of American beer. When the weekly ration was sold out, there were two choices: switch to wine or "green" Mexican beer from such brands as Cruze Blanca, Carta Blanca, Tecata, San Luis or Topaz. Beer bottles were in short supply for the Mexican breweries and any bottle capable of holding a standard bottle cap was put to use. It was not uncommon to drink Mexican beer out of a ketchup bottle. A few people reverted back to making their own homebrew.

When Texas lawmakers passed the Local Option Liquor Law in 1960 several liquor stores quickly emerged in Mingus. These stores did about a half million dollars in yearly sales and cut deeply into some Fort Worth liquor businesses. This prompted one large Fort Worth liquor retailer to open a store in Mingus.

There were several killings: Manny Nichols, Big Tony Luadi, Jenny Moore, Cub Meneghetti and Red Gobel. One man was beaten to death with a tire tool in a fight over a bottle of grappo. There were several knifings and many fights. Mingus got a reputation as a tough town. If one were looking for trouble, he could be accommodated. Today, with improved communications and transportation, there is little trouble.

With beer, live country music and ghosts of the past the little town of 300 swells to a 1,000 on Saturday night. In the fall of 1981 the Texas Tourist Development Agency determined that "Mingus on Saturday night" ranked nineteenth in the state as a tourist attraction. Surrounding towns might prefer a "dry" environment. But leading citizens of these "dry towns" are often seen in Mingus, imbibing and enjoying what Thurber-Mingus has offered for over a hundred years.

MONEY PROCEDURES IN THURBER

*I*t is astonishing that Thurber, with a work force of 3,000 and a population of 6,000, had no bank, only a Cashier and Paymaster in the person of T. R. Hall. To conduct its business the Company used the First National Bank of Dallas. As for the residents of Thurber, there was no need for a bank, for Thurber was a typical Company Town, and the Texas and Pacific Coal Company owned everything: houses, utilities, stores, churches, etc. There was no need for loans to buy or repair a house or buy land or open a business. For immediate money needs within the confines of Thurber, the Company would advance "check" (scrip) against wages in $1 to $10 booklets. This scrip was good in any Thurber store and discouraged outside purchases, even though goods were often cheaper from outside peddlers and stores. But once enmeshed in the "check" system, it was hard to extricate oneself and get back to a cash basis.

The foreign-born of Thurber did not trust banks and sometimes buried money in canning jars. When the Italians sent money back to the "Old Country," whether subsistence for family or for passage money to America, they used a New York firm "Cantoni & Co," which had ties to a Milan, Italy bank. But after about 1910 the Texas and Pacific Coal Co. provided this service in conjunction with a Milan, Italy bank.

In 1907 Joe Abraham, a Lebanese merchant in suburban Thurber Junction, organized the Thurber Junction State Bank. When Thurberites had special banking needs, this nearby bank was available. This bank existed as long as Thurber, but failed in June 1930 under mysterious circumstances, notwithstanding the fact that this was the time of the Great Depression when banks were failing all over the country.

**JOHN AUDA OF THURBER, TEXAS SENT A
DRAFT TO ITALY BY CANTONI AND CO. OF NEW YORK**

**THURBER HAD NO BANK, SO
THURBERITES USED THE BANK IN NEARBY THURBER JUNCTION**

Shortly before the bank failed Henry Rucker, long-time bank cashier, was found dead at the bottom of a cistern across the street from the bank, behind Peretti's garage. There was blunt trauma to the head, but the brief investigation concluded "accidental death!"

Some rumors: Mr. Rucker was distraught over the bank's condition and committed suicide by drowning himself.

Mr. Rucker was "done in" because he threatened to reveal the real cause of the bank's difficulties to Bank Examiners.

A prominent citizen had a large, fraudulent note outstanding and feared exposure.

Henry Rucker was a religious, loving family man, and the family knew he would never commit suicide. They pushed for a thorough investigation of his death, but there was little money and not the right connections, so the matter was dropped.

The visionary merchant/banker Joe Abraham died in 1934 after losing thousands of dollars in this bank and bad customer credit.

In July 1913 T. R. Hall, Cashier and Paymaster at Thurber, gave a "Twenty-fifth Anniversary" paper which summarized Texas and Pacific Coal Company operations. Mr. Hall, who went to work for the company in 1889, had first-hand knowledge of events which shaped the Company. A portion of Mr. Hall's paper is presented here to show how some money was handled in Thurber, i.e., the "merchandise coupon system" (check). Hall's paper also tells of the 1894 train robbery of Thurber's pay day funds wherein T and P's fiery President Hunter quickly had a posse on the robbers' trail.

An interesting sequel to the above events is a chapter from the book by Texas Ranger Sergeant W.J.P. Sullivan. This account gives an example of Hunter's irascibility which evolved into a lusty brawl in Thurber. It also emphasizes Hunter's reliance on the Texas Rangers.

T. R. HALL'S 1913 REPORT ON THURBER

"...I served as helper to the carpenters for several months, fired a boiler at Mine No. 2. I served as helper for two months, when I was promoted to weigh master at No. 2 and served in this capacity until September 1891, when I was promoted to the position of check clerk in the Mining Office, and in May 1895, I was appointed Cashier and Paymaster, my present position.

In the beginning of the company's operations it was necessary to have a system of accounting and handling accounts of miners; Mr. Edgar L. Marston, then Treasurer of the company, had this in charge and among other things he instituted the merchandise coupon system, which covered every detail for which it was intended so completely that it has been in vogue here for twenty-five years, with practically no change in style of check book, or in the method of their use.

Pay Days: Under this head, I wish to say that in the beginning, Colonel Hunter set the third Saturday of each month as Pay Day. This day was used until August, 1904, when the agreement signed at Pittsburgh, Kansas, with the United Mine Workers of America provided that Pay Days be the first and third Saturdays of each month, and during all the twenty-five years operations, the company has only failed once to meet its pay day on the specified date.

This was in November, 1894, and was caused by an attempt to rob the train on the Friday before pay day. It was known that the funds for meeting the miners' pay day were being shipped on that day, and the robbers stationed themselves about one and one half miles east of Gordon, captured a section gang and had them take up a rail and flag the train. There were four of them, and when the train stopped, two of them boarded the express car while the other two stood guard and kept the passengers inside the coaches. The express manager convinced them that he could not open the safe, so they undertook to dynamite it with the result that the door was sprung so badly that they could not open it, and had to abandon the attempt. They took all the money that was kept outside of the main safe, which was considerable, it being cotton season and much money was being shipped to the local stations for the purpose of buying cotton. This money was kept in an iron box and was convenient for the express manager to open on its arrival at stations. This they appropriated. The exact amount has never been known, but it was variously estimated at from five to forty thousand dollars. The Texas & Pacific Coal Company's pay funds, in the safe, amounted to thirty-three thousand dollars.

Owing to the damage done to the safe it could not be opened for several days and as a result pay day was postponed until the following Wednesday, during which time the company shipped other funds from Fort Worth.

As soon as Colonel Hunter was advised that the train had been robbed, he started a posse in pursuit, headed by Captain William Lightfoot, Grude Britton and Lit Williams. The robbers went north from where they undertook to rob the train, cutting fences and keeping as straight a course as possible, heading for the mountainous country fifteen miles away. The robbery occurred at one o'clock in the afternoon, and at three o'clock the same afternoon the posse started by Colonel Hunter took up their trail, and followed it until dark. On resuming their chase next morning, they found where the robbers had camped the night before and divided their loot; a number of money bags and other papers scattered about on the ground indicated this. This occurred in a cave in the mountain-side at a place called Board Tree Spring. From there the robbers scattered and all trace of them was lost; however, the hunt was kept up and Colonel Hunter always thought, and I believe he was right, that Ben and Jim Hughes, two notorious characters who formerly lived in Palo Pinto County, planned the robbery.

Ben Hughes lived in what was then known as the Indian Territory; and officers heard that he had a gang around him there, who were supposed to be the men who robbed the Texas & Pacific train. Colonel Hunter sent Captain Lightfoot, Britton, Williams and Sam Farmer, formerly a policeman at Fort Worth, to Hughes' place in the Territory. They secured an Indian policeman to help, as a guide and to make the arrest. They went to the house kept by Ben Hughes, nine miles from the station, at night, and surrounded it, thinking to wait until daylight and arrest him and his gang when they came out in the morning. Just before daylight, however, a dog belonging to the premises discovered the presence of the men and was so vicious that Sam Farmer had to shoot it. This stampeded the men in the house and they came out shooting their Winchesters, and the fight commenced in the dark. When daylight came it was found that the Indian policeman was dead, having been shot through the head, and Ben Hughes with his right arm broken from a bullet was lying behind a log, begging the boys not to shoot him. However, his wife stood over him with a Winchester and refused to let the officers come near him until they promised to let her go with him. The other men who were in the house, four in number, escaped.

The boys loaded the dead Indian and Hughes, with his wife, in a farm wagon and took them to the station. Ben was brought to trial in Dallas, in the United States District Court, and acquitted by proving an alibi. We afterwards learned that the men who were in that house that night were the men who robbed the Texas and Pacific Train on November 16th, the year before, and we think were then making plans to come to Thurber and rob us on pay day. Colonel Hunter, right in the beginning, started the custom of sending a heavy guard to the station to receive the funds for pay day, and it has been kept up to the present time, and this has perhaps saved us from being robbed a number of times...

TWELVE YEARS IN THE SADDLE
FOR LAW AND ORDER
ON THE
FRONTIERS OF TEXAS
BY SERGEANT W. J. L. SULLIVAN
Texas Ranger
Co B, Frontier Battalion
X
AN EXCITING FISTICUFF

Col. R. D. Hunter wrote to Capt. S. A. McMurray of our company, asking him to let me have a leave of absence to go to Thurber to attend to some anarchists and dynamiters, who were giving the officials a lot of trouble at the mine. He said, in his letter to Capt. McMurray, that he would give me a hundred dollars a month to act as an officer of the company and rid the mine of these characters.

The Captain showed me the letter and asked me if I thought I could do the work. I told him that I was perfectly confident that I could. He then asked me if I wanted to go and try it, and I told him that hundred dollars looked mighty good to me. He gave me permission to go, and I left on the next train for Thurber, and I reached there as quickly as possible and made a contract with Hunter to do the work which he had mapped out for me. I remained in the employ of the coal company eight months.

One night, about twelve o'clock, I located thirteen anarchists in one bunch, hidden in a little dark corner planning to dynamite the mine the following night. I had two men with me, and we crawled up close enough to hear every word that these anarchists said. When they had perfected their plans and stopped their discussion, we arrested the whole bunch and jailed them.

A saloon was run at the mines by Tom Lawson, who had a ten-year lease on the building. Lawson also owned a fourth interest in the mine, but he and Col. Hunter, the president, had a falling out for some cause, and Lawson got to standing in with the tough element. One night I heard a pistol shot in the saloon and ran in there to investigate believing that somebody had been killed. When I reached the inside, I learned that Lawson, who was behind the bar drunk, had shot at a miner, but failed to hit him. This was on pay night and everybody was full of beer and whiskey, and I had already filled the calaboose with drunken men.

I decided to arrest Lawson and put him in with the other men, but when I advanced on him he made a play for his six shooter, but I fell squarely on top of him with my gun, removing enough skin from his head to half-sole a number 10 shoe. He swore that he would not be locked up, but I put him in the calaboose, all the same, and he was made to pay his fine as any other man. After paying his fine, Lawson left immediately to report me to Capt. McMurray. Col. Hunter saw Lawson in Fort Worth looking for McMurray and wired me about it, saying that he would stand between me and all danger.

About two weeks after that Capt. McMurray came to Thurber and told me that he understood that I had knocked Lawson in the head and, and that he wanted to know the cause of it. I told him that Lawson was disturbing the peace and that he had shot at a miner, and when I tried to arrest him he attempted to draw a gun on me, and that I hit him with my six shooter instead of shooting him with it. "I disarmed him and put him in jail," I continued, and my Captain replied that I ought to have broken his neck. About two months after that, Lawson and his bartender, Malcom, and Col. Hunter, all three met in the drug store. Hunter and Lawson began cursing each other, and I heard the row and rushed into the store just in time to see Hunter burst the bottom of a spittoon out over Tom Lawson's head. Hunter then threw a box of cigars at him, striking Lawson in the ear and scattering cigars all over the floor. I noticed Malcom slipping up behind Col. Hunter, preparing to hit him in the back of the head. Just as he started to strike Hunter, however, I struck Malcom myself, in time to stop what would have been a dreadful blow. Malcom whirled around and saw that it was I who hit him. I struck him five times in the face, but he did nothing but back off the gallery. I struck him once again when he reached the outside and kicked him off the gallery. I thought I had him whipped, but when he got up he said he would fight me if I would pull my six shooter off. He was a stout man and weighed about 230 pounds, but I was not afraid of him. I removed my six shooter and threw it over to Henry Kronk, the druggist, and told him to look out for it. I then pitched into Malcom again, striking him in the face. He suddenly threw his big arm around my neck and pressed my head against his body. I could not get my head free without breaking my neck, and, having the advantage of me in that respect, he commenced beating my head, nose and eyes until my face looked like jelly. I do not know what would have become of my face if Bob Ward, the company's lawyer, had not come to my rescue. Ward knocked Malcom loose from me and knocked him twelve feet from where we were clinched. Tom Lawson then knocked Ward down, he falling on top of Malcom. Hunter was pacing around after Lawson with a heavy rock, but never did get in his lick.

When a carpenter, who was working near by, saw the dangerous position that I was in when Malcom had me clinched, he ran to my rescue with a hatchet in his hand. He was frightened and as pale as death, and he intended to cut Malcom loose with his hatchet, but Ward got in ahead of him and did the work for him.

My face was in a terrible fix, and the doctor put a beef steak on it to draw the blood out of the bruised places. My face was so badly bruised and swollen that one could hardly tell where my eyes and nose were. I had a girl then, whom I loved very dearly, and I could not go to see her for a long time, on account of the sad condition of my complexion. I shunned her everywhere for quite a while; for I well knew that it would never do to let "Betty" see me in that fix.

I went to the Justice of Peace the next morning after the fight and paid my fine, which amounted to twelve dollars. The money was paid back to me by Col. Hunter. Hunter, Ward, Malcom and Lawson all fought their cases hard, but it cost them about two hundred dollars apiece before they were through, while the fight only cost me twelve dollars, and the money was refunded to me.

THE RAILROADS' IMPORTANCE
IN THURBER

In Thurber's days, the railroad touched the lives of everyone, for the people depended on the railroad for travel, commerce, mail, shipping and jobs. The railroad needed Thurber coal, and Thurber needed the railroad to ship coal and bricks, to transport people and to receive goods.

W.W. Johnson's first coal mine in northern Erath County was 2-½ miles south of the main east-west rail line of Jay Gould's Texas and Pacific Railroad. Coal was desperately needed by the railroad, and in 1887 the railroad built a spur to the Johnson Mine.[1] The spur connected to the main line with a "Y", so coal cars could be more conveniently handled, heading east or west. And this juncture with the main line was located 3 miles west of Gordon and 5 miles east of Strawn. Initially, there was no settlement at this juncture, and the railroaders called this "Coal Mine Junction."[2]

In 1888 R.D. Hunter's Texas and Pacific Coal Co. (no connection to the railroad) bought Johnson's coal interests and the coal camp was named "Thurber." And "Coal Mine Junction" became "Thurber Junction." But railroaders called this "The Junction."[3] And during Prohibition (1920-1933) Thurber Junction was jokingly called "Grappo Junction" because it was a bootlegging center known for its grappo (grape) Italian whiskey.[4]

About 1895, with increased passenger traffic and coal shipments, a community began to grow around Thurber Junction and a wooden depot was built. The name hung on the depot was "Mingus," after an early settler. But in reality, there were two communities. North of the tracks was "Mingus" where all homes and businesses were owned by Americans. South of the tracks many homes and businesses were owned by immigrants.[5] Since the railroad spur was south of the main line, this was where many interesting aspects of railroading took place. There was a rail car repair barn with five storage tracks a quarter-mile south of the depot.[6] Boxcars and coal cars were stored here, and this is where the Italians received their boxcar loads of California grapes to make wine. Several times a day, a coal train would go back and forth between Thurber and the Junction, and kids would sometimes hop a ride. There was a sand car a few hundred yards south of the depot where kids played.[7] The engines used the sand for traction. There was a section gang storage barn on the west part of the "Y" and a friendly foreman, "Buster" Vinson, let the boys play on the pump cart. And one time he came charging down the line, terrified that the boys had gotten on the main line with the cart.[8]

Railroad pocket watches were highly prized (they were more reliable), and when the passenger/mail trains pulled in, men would get out their watches to check on its time. It seemed like a contest between the engineer and the "watchers."

It was only after Thurber began its decline in the 1920s when the name "Thurber Junction" faded away too, so that today this location is called "Mingus."

The railroad spur was the artery of Thurber's being. Although Thurber was only 2-1/2 miles south of the main line, there were about twenty miles of track throughout Thurber territory.[9] Thurber's coal veins extended westward about eight miles. But the tracks took a circuitous route to each mine before reaching the furthest mine. And there were storage tracks, passing tracks and run-around tracks. Provisions were offloaded directly from railcars to the grocery store, the lumber yard and the Snake Saloon. The train carried miners to work and back each day and coal cars to and from the mines. Peak coal production was in 1915 when 19,200 coal cars were shipped.[10] But coal was just a part of the picture. Brick production was 80,000 bricks a day and there were four sub-rail spurs to the brickyard.

There were also tracks to the foundry, the cotton gin and the lumber yard. Whiskey could be ordered by telegram or mail and shipped parcel post. Sears Roebuck and Montgomery Ward catalogue mail orders did a brisk business; packages were shipped parcel post.

The wealthy had private rail cars, and they could travel anywhere in the country. There was a double track through downtown Thurber, and the private cars of Jay Gould, Edgar Marston, VIPs and opera troupes would sometimes be parked on the second track. Lottie Bielinski remembers that in 1906 the company gave the kids in Thurber a free train ride to Thurber Junction to visit the Mingus Little Lake Recreational Area.[11]

Thurber train passengers entrained and detrained at the Mingus Depot. Passenger trains were met by a concord stage from Thurber's Knox Hotel which was driven by Frank Whitworth. This was the last regularly scheduled stagecoach run in America.[12] In 1906 the Mingus Depot burned and a new attractive brick depot was built. The depot was the busiest between Fort Worth and El Paso. At its peak, monthly ticket sales averaged $100,000. just for the eastbound passengers.[13] The Mingus depot was in sharp contrast to the depots at nearby Gordon and Strawn which were plain wood structures and painted the railroad's bland yellow. Today, the brick depot at Ranger is still in use, not as a depot, but as an oil museum. The brick work in the Ranger Depot would compare with the Mingus Depot. The Mingus Depot was torn down about 1950, but no one remembers who tore it down, or what happened to the bricks. The wooden depot presently in Thurber is not a part of Thurber. This is the depot from Strawn which was moved to Thurber in the 1960s.

The railroads sometimes ran "specials" for certain events, such as the Fort Worth Fat Stock Shows and passenger trains made stops at every little town, as necessary, to pick up or discharge passengers. The writer remembers accompanying his mother several times on the train from Mingus to Strawn, a five-mile trip.

Thurber coal helped open up the southwest by providing the railroads a reliable coal supply for thirty-three years. When the Texas & Pacific RR began expanding westward, most coal came from Indian Territory (Oklahoma). The coal supply became more crucial the farther west the rails went, not to be solved until the discovery of Thurber coal. While the T & P RR was the chief purchaser of Thurber coal, there were a dozen other RRs using Thurber coal, such as International & Great Northern Ry Co, Ft. Worth & Rio Grande Ry Co., Texas Central Ry Co., St. Louis & Southwestern Ry Co., Stephenville, N & S Texas Ry Co., W.M.W. & N.W. Ry Co., Texas & Brazos Valley Ry Co., Texas Southeastern Ry, Abilene & Southern Ry, and Texas State Ry Co.[14]

Thurber Junction/Mingus was a coaling/watering/rest stop where the trains refueled and passengers were given twenty minutes to eat in restaurants near the depot. Some of the restaurants were run by Jester, Bostick, Deaton, Wells and Minyard.[15] Near the Mingus depot the Thurber Coal Company owned the Junction Hotel, which also had a dining room. The Junction Hotel accommodated those Thurber visitors who had to remain overnight or who failed to make train connections.

In Mingus there were section gang houses west of the depot where Mexican workers lived.[16] Another section gang house was located about 10 miles east at Judd Switch. To work for the railroad on a train crew, or as a depot agent/telegrapher, or in the car yards, was a first-rate job. Bud Tucker, the Mingus Depot Agent, became a legend in the T & P RR, having worked for this railroad 64 years, starting at age 14 and retiring at age 78.[17] The agent/telegrapher held an enviable position, for he was the first to get outside news. Although Thurber did not have a depot, it did have a telegrapher (Ike Newman) to handle its business communications. The coal chute and watering tank for the train locomotives were east of the Mingus depot. The coal chute was about 30 feet high, and kids used to climb up the coal chute timbers to catch roosting pigeons.[18] The coal chute was torn down in the late 1920s, but the concrete water tank still stands.

In 1913 a coal chute worker, St. Clair, was working the night shift. He lived about 70 yards from the coal chute. He went home about 2 A.M. to get his lunch. Later, when he finished his night shift, he came home to find his daughter, wife and mother-in-law bludgeoned to death. He was a suspect but was never indicted. This was known as the 1913 Triple Murder.[19]

During the Great Depression of the 1930s, each freight train would have dozens of hoboes who "rode the rails," seeking work in different parts of the country. Most of these were good men, willing to work, and they were able to hitch a free but uncomfortable and dangerous ride aboard the freight. But sometimes they encountered a mean "bull" (railroad detective) that would be downright cruel by physically kicking hoboes off moving trains, resulting in injury or even death.

One man who rode the freights told of his trouble with a mean "bull." "He wouldn't let me hop the train; he pistol whipped me and cussed me out. I didn't give him any sass, all I was trying to do was to get to my next job. He was still around the next day, so I looked for freight just about dark. I waited for the train to get moving good, then I picked up a 4 x 4 timber and hit that S.O.B. right across the side of the head and then I hopped the train. To this day I don't know whether I killed him or what."[20]

During the Depression Years of 1933-1940, when the freight trains made fueling stops in Mingus, dozens of hoboes would quickly fan out all over town, seeking a bite to eat. If a "bull" kept them from hopping back aboard, or if they missed the train, they stayed in a "hobo jungle" on Gibson Creek near the water tower. Their fires for cooking and/or warmth could be seen at night. Most townspeople kept watchdogs and loaded shotguns, but there were few instances of stealing property, for there was no way a hobo could escape.

In 1938 a Negro hobo was killed trying to hop freight. No identification to queries sent up and down the line. Mingus had two cemeteries, both private. This meant no place to bury a Negro. Consequently, he was buried just outside the entrance to the Woodmen of the World Cemetery on the east side of town.

In a recorded interview in 1991, Joe Beacham age 96, who was on a mine train crew in Thurber made some interesting observations about trains and other events in Thurber. His memory at this age was remarkable.[21]

He lived in house #77, a green house. His father worked in the Brick Yard, and Joe also worked in the Brick Yard from 1910-1913. He operated the pug mill, a machine that mixed the powdered shale and water for paving bricks. He went to work for the railroad in 1913 on a mine train crew.

There were section gang houses on Polander Hill for Mexicans who worked on the tracks to the mines. Beacham's train once killed three cows near Turkey Creek (near #7 Mine). The Mexican Section gang workers loaded the cows on a RR hand pump cart and hauled them to their houses which were right next to the RR track. They butchered the cows and sliced the meat into strips which they spread all around their houses to dry into jerky – clothes lines, fences, porch rails etc. It was summer, and plenty of sunshine to cure the meat.

On Thurber being a strong union town after the 1903 strike: "I believe it was the Grocery Store that burned down about 1906. When they went to build a new store, the bricks didn't have the union symbol, so the bricklayers wouldn't lay the bricks. They finally got bricks with the union label and the store was finally built."

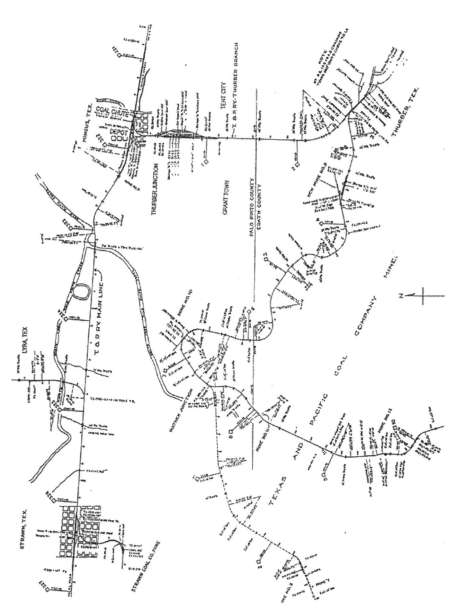

JUNE 4, 1918 RAIL LINES IN/NEAR THURBER

In 1918 or 1919, Joe was on his way to work. There was a big thunderstorm. Lightning hit the bell tower of the Christian Church which was located next to the RR track on the way up to Polander-Italian Hill. The bell gave one real loud gong, and the church caught fire. By the time Joe's train passed the site 30 minutes later, there was nothing but smoking embers left.

For a year or so, there was train passenger service to Thurber. The train got off the main line at Thurber Junction and onto the Thurber Spur. There were two trains a day, one eastbound and one westbound. Trains often turned around by using the "Y" at Thurber Junction.

Joe Beacham was transferred from a Thurber train crew to a Ranger train crew in 1919 when the Oil Boom was on. Several years later, his train was at the Thurber Brick Yard (probably to get bricks for Ranger). While at the Brick Yard, he recognized a Negro man and went over to warmly greet him, "Uncle Albert!" And the black man said, "I thought that was you, 'Young Beacham'." "Uncle Albert" was Albert Whitehead, a happy, well-liked brick yard worker. (Whitehead died in 1962 at the age of 98.) Later, Beacham's co-workers criticized Beacham for his show of affection for a Negro, saying, "Around here we don't shake hands with Negroes." And Joe Beacham said, "Let me tell you boys a story."

"When I was about eight or nine, each day I'd take my Daddy's lunch to him at the Brick Yard. One day I hitched a ride on one of the electric cars that carried the brick into the kilns. The axle I was standing on rotated with the wheels, and somehow this flipped me under the car, and I was being dragged to a crossing where I would be crushed to death. Albert Whitehead saw my danger, and jerked the jumper off the electric wire, stopping the train, and thereby saving my life."

"At home that evening my Daddy said he wasn't going to spank me; he was just glad I wasn't killed. But he wanted me to go thank

Albert Whitehead for saving my life. This I did, and after that Albert called me 'Young Beacham,' and I called him 'Uncle Albert'."

"Now boys," he said to his co-workers, "if you were me, would you shake Uncle Albert's hand?"

"Hell, we would have hugged and kissed him."

(Joe Beacham died about two months after this interview.)

THE RAILROADS' IMPORTANCE IN THURBER NOTES

1. Willie M. Floyd, "Thurber, Texas: An Abandoned Coal Field Town," Dallas: Master's Thesis, SMU, June 1939, p. 23.

2. Leo S. Bielinski, Book Review of John S. Spratt's Thurber, Texas, Abilene: West Texas Historical Assn. Year Book, Vol. LXIII, 1987, p. 244.

3. Western Union Telegram, Sept 22, 1889, to Charles W. Moore, Thurber, Texas from J. W. Davis (Author's personal collection).

4. Leo S. Bielinski, "Beer, Booze, Bootlegging and Bocci Ball in Thurber-Mingus," Abilene: West TX Historical Assn Year Book, Vol. LIX, 1983, p. 78.

5. Bielinski, Book Review, p. 245.

6. Texas and Pacific Ry, Map of Mines and Tracks near Mingus & Strawn, Texas, Dallas: June 4th 1918 (Author's Personal Collection).

7. Albert Abraham, Interview, Mingus, Texas: December 1995.

8. Ibid.

9. Texas and Pacific Ry. Map (Numbers by squares indicate mileage).

10. Willie M. Floyd, "Thurber, Texas," p. 82.

11. Lottie Bielinski Conversation, Mingus Texas: One of many between 1985-1987. Mrs. Bielinski was born in Thurber, 1898.

12. Fort Worth Star Telegram, Ed Brice Column, date unknown. Bernice Bearden Personal Collection, Mingus, TX 76463

13. John S. Spratt, <u>Thurber, Texas</u>, Austin: U of Texas Press, 1986, p. 119.

14. Texas and Pacific Coal Co. "Cash Receipts & Disbursements, Thurber: Dec 1911," (Copy in Author's Personal Collection).

15. John S. Spratt, <u>Thurber, Texas</u>, p. 69.

16. Albert Abraham Interview, Dec 1995.

17. Leo S. Bielinski, Book Review, p. 246.

18. Albert Abraham Interview, Dec 1995.

19. Leo S. Bielinski, Book Review, p. 246.

20. Anonymous Interviewee, Mingus, Texas: Nov 1962. (Anonymity because of involvement).

21. Joe Beacham, Taped Interview, Fort Worth: 9 March 1991. (Author's Possession).

THE 1903 THURBER MINERS' MEETING AT ROCKY CREEK BRIDGE AND ITS SIGNIFICANCE IN THE SOUTHWEST LABOR MOVEMENT

One of the most dramatic scenes in American labor took place on Thursday September 10, 1903 at the little one-lane bridge at Rocky Creek in southern Palo Pinto County, Texas. About 300 miners from the United Mine Workers Local at Lyra marched four miles eastward to Rocky Creek to meet a thousand miners and other workers from Thurber who had marched four miles northward through Thurber Junction to this midway meeting place. The multi-ethnic miners from Thurber were unofficially on strike but not yet union members.

The Fort Worth Telegram, 10 September 1903, reported "A big mass meeting was held today in a grove midway between Lyra and Thurber. Every employee of the Thurber mines was present and yesterday and today 1,057 joined the union." And the following day the Telegram related that "The meeting of the miners yesterday was held in a grove three miles from Lyra, half way between this place and Thurber...The miners from here went to the grove to meet those coming from Thurber. They marched 287 strong...At the meeting there were at least 1,500 men...The English speaking people predominated...There are 102 Mexicans, about 200 Italians, and 120 Poles. The rest are Americans, except twenty Negroes."[2]

The Dallas Morning News, story dateline 10 September 1903, reported "During the forenoon today the miners held a meeting at the Rock(sic) Creek Bridge, about a mile below Thurber Junction and four miles from Thurber."[3] These first newspaper accounts give clear indication this meeting was held at or near Rocky Creek Bridge which was about equidistance from Lyra and Thurber by the roads existing at the time.[4] With 287 of their Lyra brethren witnessing and offering encouragement, the Union Oath was administered to several hundred more miners, and then National Organizer W. M. Wardjon spoke on unionism and the upcoming strike. "He spoke through interpreters to the Italians, Poles and Mexicans and without an interpreter to the English-speaking workingmen."[5] Mr. Woodman, Secretary of the State Federation of Labor, 60,000 strong assured the miners his organization would back the miners. "These announcements, as well as many others, and a song by Mr. Wardjon, composed by himself, and entitled 'The Miner's Battle Song,' caused much cheering."[6] This emotional, eventful meeting at Rocky Creek Bridge ensured strength, solidarity and success for the 1903 Thurber Coal Miners' Strike which had a consequential effect on the labor movement in the Southwest.[7] With its 1,000 miners Thurber was the "Plum"[8] for the union because transportation and commerce depended on coal, and Thurber coal fueled Texas and Pacific RR, the main route across Texas, and provided coal for several other railroads as well.[9]

However, as momentous and historic as the Thursday September 10, 1903 Rocky Creek meeting was, subsequent accounts of this event, while referring to the first three references above, give confused views on the specific location of the meeting. For example, one writer quoted the Dallas paper almost verbatim: "During the forenoon of September 10, the miners held a meeting at Rock(sic) Creek Bridge about one mile below Thurber Junction and four miles from Thurber."[10] A second writer stated that when the miners' demands were refused, "The miners again marched over the hills to Lyra where more than 1,000 men repeated the oath of the UMW. The meeting was held beneath the railroad bridge over Rock(sic) Creek, midway between Strawn and Mingus."[11] A third writer entirely rejected the September 10, Rocky Creek meeting and wrote that when the miners' demands were refused, "the miners boycotted the mines the following day (Wed., Sep 9), marched to Lyra and congregated in a grove. Several hundred miners joined the union on the spot, and organizers called another meeting to be held at the Palo Pinto Bridge. On Friday unionized miners led the procession and upon arrival at the bridge…"[12] Another writer reported: The union delegates called another mass meeting for the following morning (Sept. 10) at the Palo Pinto Bridge, approximately half way between Lyra and Thurber."[13] (Palo Pinto Bridge was 3 miles from Thurber and 4 miles from Lyra.) There were several subsequent meetings for various purposes. For example, there was an assembly at Grant Town, which was just outside Hunter's damnable barb wire fence.[14] "The meeting of the miners today (Rocky Creek) was held off the company's property. That which has been called for tomorrow (Fri. Sept. 11) will be held on a three acre tract belonging to a Mr. Wilson, who has joined the union. It has been described as being located in the 'suburbs' of Thurber."[15] This meeting instructed families on how to leave Thurber, and newspaper pictures show many women in attendance.[16] On September 12, there was a meeting at the Palo Pinto Creek Bridge wherein the last of the miners, sixty-three, joined the union, and C. W. Woodman organized Thurber's brick and icemen.[17] Another meeting at Grant Town was on Monday September 14, when Mrs. Lamphere organized the company clerks. Barbers and bartenders also sought unionization at this time.[18]

In the beginning miners were timid and fearful of company retribution and distanced their meetings well away from Thurber. But as the miners became more organized they became bolder, and meetings edged closer to Thurber. The first two organizational meetings were at Lyra, eight miles from Thurber. The third was at Rocky Creek about four miles from Thurber. Then, Palo Pinto Creek Bridge, three miles from Thurber. And finally at Grant Town which was just outside Thurber's barb wire fence.

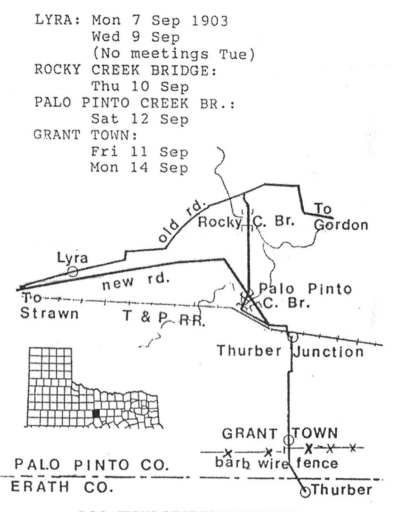

```
LYRA: Mon 7 Sep 1903
      Wed 9 Sep
      (No meetings Tue)
ROCKY CREEK BRIDGE:
      Thu 10 Sep
PALO PINTO CREEK BR.:
      Sat 12 Sep
GRANT TOWN:
      Fri 11 Sep
      Mon 14 Sep
```

**LOCATIONS OF UNION MEETINGS –
1903 MINERS' STRIKE**

At this time the United Mine Works already had locals at nearby Strawn and Lyra and at the Rock Creek Mines east of Mineral Wells.[19] But Thurber's Texas and Pacific Coal Company (no connection to T & P RR) had an absolute nonunion camp ever since R. D. Hunter took over the mines in 1888 and broke the local Knights of Labor. And to enforce his nonunion policy, Hunter encircled Thurber with a barb wire fence to keep out labor agitators.[20] Miners suspected of union membership were summarily dismissed, and union organizers were ceremoniously beaten up and dumped outside the company gate.[21] Another problem in organizing was finding interpreters for a dozen ethnic groups. Tony Gardetto translated for the miners at Rocky Creek in Italian, French and Spanish.[22]

Hunter died in 1902, a year before the pivotal strike, but his resolute nonunion policy was reiterated again on August 23, 1903 when "...posters were placed in conspicuous places throughout the camp, in which the declaration was made that none but nonunion miners shall be employed in the Thurber mines."[23] After the strike was settled on 27 September 1903, several interesting side issues evolved. Thurber became the first totally unionized city in America.[24] New employees had to apply for union membership within 24 hours.[25] The brick workers gained approval to put their union logo on each brick made in Thurber, an imbedded triangle with the letter "B" at one vertex, and a "T" at each other point: Brick, Tile and Terra cotta workers. Hunter's barb wire fence came down. Workers were no longer "locked in" to a scrip money system and company stores, but could now trade with outside merchants and farmers.

Although the foreign-born comprised 80% of the miners, they were not appointed to any union positions and their grievances were ignored. In 1906 the Italian miners threatened to join the socialist-leaning I.W.W. (wobblies), and the UMW quickly granted a second charter in Thurber, the "Italian" Local #2753. All immigrant European miners, Mexicans and blacks joined, and this local was several times larger than the original UMW Local #2538.[26]

Thurber prospered until 1921. But by this time most railroads had switched to oil, and coal was no longer profitable.

Contrary to a popular view, it was not a strike that killed the Thurber mines. The company reneged on its last union contract and "locked out" the miners.[27] There was no severance pay, no unemployment pay, and no retirement pay. Miners and their families again were forced to vacate their Thurber homes and moved into surplus WWI tents at "Tent City," a half mile north of Thurber.[28] Bootlegging enabled many ex-miners to survive the hard times. Again, contrary to popular belief, Thurber did not cease mining coal at this time. There were still contracts for coal, and #10 and New #3 mines continued to operate until 1926 with a mixture of "scab" and union labor.[29] But the UMW was no longer a force. The Lyra mines continued until after WWII. There was a surplus of miners, and "scab" was a word which would provoke a fight among school kids when one called the other's dad the hated word.[30]

There were three attempts to operate small family coal mines in Grant Town: the Obels, Greens and Gazzolas, but these were not profitable.[31] Although the Thurber coal vein averages only twenty-eight inches, there are an estimated 127,000,000 tons of coal left underground at Thurber.[32]

Today, 90 years after the electrified days which began on Labor Day, 1903 and culminated with the beginning of the Labor Movement in the Southwest, most of the landmarks of that time are gone. Thurber is a ghost town. There is no trace of Lyra. The first Palo Pinto Creek Bridge, part of the original road to Lyra/Strawn, and which crossed the creek in a NE-SW direction, was scrapped around 1930. The road over which the miners marched from Lyra to Rocky Creek Bridge has been blotted out with cactus and mesquite. About 1920 a new Thurber Junction-Lyra/Strawn road was built which entirely by-passed Rocky Creek. And an important labor historical site was forgotten. But the little bridge over Rocky Creek is still intact; its role in the 1903 strike perhaps ignored, but it continues to function as part of a county road used by ranchers and oil operators.

THE 1903 THURBER MINERS' MEETING NOTES

1. <u>Fort Worth Telegram</u>, September 10, 1903.

2. <u>Fort Worth Telegram</u>, September 11, 1903.

3. <u>Dallas Morning News</u>, September 11, 1903.

4. US Geological Survey Map, 1891. Also Tony Sadver to Leo S. Bielinski, Strawn, TX. June 1991, interview.

5. <u>Dallas Morning News</u>, September 11, 1903.

6. Ibid.

7. Leo S. Bielinski, <u>The Back Road to Thurber</u>, Baird, TX: Joy Presswork Collection, 1993, X.

8. Richard Mason, VCR, "Boom Town to Ghost Town," Gordon, TX Thurber Historical Association, 1991.

9. T & P Coal Co. & T P M & M Co., "Statement of Operations and Trial Balance 1898," Thurber, Texas.

10. Mary Jane Gentry, "Thurber: the Life and Death of a Texas Town" (M.A. Thesis University of Texas, 1946), 80.

11. Weldon B. Hardman, <u>Fire in a Hole!</u> (Gordon, TX: Thurber Historical Association, 1991), 47.

12. Marilyn D. Rhinehart, "Underground Patriots: Thurber Coal Miners and the Struggle for Individual Freedom 1888-1903," <u>Southwestern Historical Quarterly</u>, XCII (Apr., 1989), 537.

13. James C. Maroney, "The Unionization Thurber, 1903," <u>Red River Valley Historical Review</u> (Spring 1979), 30.

14. <u>Dallas Morning News</u>, September 13, 1903.

15. <u>Dallas Morning News</u>, September 11, 1903.

16. Fort Worth Telegram, September 13, 1903.

17. Ibid.

18. Dallas Morning News, September 14, 1903.

19. Hardman, Fire in a Hole!: 44.

20. Gentry, "Thurber: Life and Death:"13.

21. Hardman, Fire in a Hole!: 44.

22. Dallas Morning News, September 14, 1903.

23. Fort Worth Telegram, September 8, 1903.

24. Hardman, Fire in a Hole!: 56.

25. W. A. Mahan, "Brick Contract September 1914-17,"(Thurber, TX: September 15, 1914): 1. (copy in possession of author).

26. Mason, in VCR, "Boom Town to Ghost Town."

27. W. K. Gordon to Edgar L. Marston, December 10, 1906. (copy in possession of author). Also Lawrence Santi to George Green, February 1974:18 (Division of Archives/manuscripts, University of Texas at Arlington).

28. Lawrence Santi to George Green: 2.

29. Lawrence Santi to George Green: 20. Also pictures of Tent City 1921 (originals in possession of author).

30. Tony Sadver to Leo S. Bielinski, Strawn, TX., June 1991, interview.

31. Ibid.

32. Gino Solignani to Leo S. Bielinski, Mingus, TX., August 1989, interview.

A MURDER IN THURBER

May 26, 1912 was "Green Sunday" (Zielone Swiatki), one of the "Old Country" customs still observed by Thurber's Poles. In America this is called Pentecost Sunday; when the Holy Ghost descended upon Earth. In Poland on this Sunday homes are decorated with greenery, such as reeds.[1] The Poles are usually a peaceful, religious people. But religion appeared to have been temporarily forgotten on this particular Sunday evening.

Pentecost Sunday begins with Mass, and there is an infusion of peace and joy for being under the guidance of the Holy Ghost. There is dinner, visiting, dancing and imbibing. But in Thurber, Texas this religious holiday in 1912 ended with a murder victim after a gang fight among six young Polish coal miners. The event was illuminated by a bright full moon and was witnessed by some fifteen Thurberites.

The ensuing murder trial was a public excitement in Thurber because homicide was such a rarity in this coal mining city of several thousand. Indeed, in forty years (1892-1932), there were only six murder cases.[2] And not all of these cases resulted in felony indictments. But in this 1912 homicide, interest was heightened because Frank Wisnoski was charged with First Degree Murder of John Czerwinski, and several witnesses knew Wisnoski was not the murderer, while others were upset by the court proceedings.

In America there has always been some prejudice against the various immigrant ("foreigner") groups, and the Stephenville Empire paper aptly illustrated this prevalent prejudice by making fun of the Polander's names. The paper reported Sheriff Deaton could not remember the names of the four Poles he took into custody on Monday 27 May 1912, saying "It was immaterial as no one getting the paper would know them anyhow."[3] And in the next issue of the

102

paper on June 7, 1912, it was facetiously reported, "No wonder Sheriff Deaton could not remember the names of the four Polanders he jailed Monday of last week ... The Thurber Journal's account supplies the missing information ... Those jailed here is Walter Cukierski, John Zeilinski, Frank W. and Tom Mulkowski."[4]

In retrospect, it appeared the Court and the State had already solved the crime, prejudged the accused and used the trial to justify their prejudgment. It seemed as if the elected officials wanted to show their toughness on crime and to teach these foreigners to obey the law. Although six people were involved in the brawl, Frank W. and Walter Cukierski *had* to be guilty because it was their bicycles which had been damaged, and the damaged bikes were purportedly the reason for the fight. This, in spite of the fact that neither man the fight, nor did testimony show that Frank W. and Cukierski ever fought with the deceased, John C. Testimony showed that Frank W.'s fight was with one Joe Sikoski; Frank W. holding Sikoski at bay with a dirk (knife). But since Frank W. was seen with a dangerous weapon (the knife), he had to be the one to charge with Murder in the First Degree! Although Sikoski was a participant in the fight, he was not jailed.

Added to all this was the question of suitable legal counsel whose ability might be suspect from his preparation of the "Assignments of Error" document in seeking a new trial. This document is replete with grammatical and spelling errors.[5] But the lawyer was probably the best Frank W. could afford. It appears defense counsel made few objections to critical points of law during the trial when Frank W. was found guilty. And while counsel did address some of these points of law during the appeals process, Frank W.'s conviction of Murder in the First Degree was upheld and he was sentenced to life.[6] Walter Cukierski, whose bicycle was also damaged prior to the fight, was convicted of manslaughter and given three years.[7] Thus, lives were ruined by a sloppy court whose interest was not justice, but rather the easiest conviction, and the actual murderer went free. But after five years in prison, the petitions "by a large number of Citizens of Erath County" and the recommendation by the Board of Pardon Advisors finally set Frank W. free on 6 July 1917.[8]

The gang fight took place near Sabota's House #540.[9] Four of the participants in the fight roomed together: Frank W., Tom Mulkowski, Walter Cukierski and John Zeilinski. Frank W. and Cukierski each owned bicycles, and someone had cut one of the bicycle tires. This act, exacerbated by emotions from too much drink, ignited a drunken brawl which was really two separate fights. Mulkowski, Cukierski and Zeilinski fought with the deceased, John C., while Frank W. tangled with Joe Sikoski.

Zeilinski testified that he was mad at the deceased, John C., because the deceased had cut Cukierski's bicycle tire. Testimony showed Zeilinski started the fight, hitting and kicking John C. "...and keeping it up until the crowd pronounced that John C. was dead."[10] Concurrently with this, a separate and distinct fight was going on between Frank W. and Joe Sikoski, an alleged bully, who had previously assaulted Frank's brother. And since Sikoski was seen earlier standing near the bicycles, Frank W. had the impression that Sikoski had cut the bicycle tire. In this fight, Frank W. pulled a knife (a dirk) to keep Sikoski at bay. Because of his small size (5' 4"),[11] a knife was probably the only way Frank W. could defend himself. The Frank W. and Sikoski fight continued until John C. in the other fight, fell to the ground. Whereupon Frank W., knife still in hand, backed off from Sikoski, went to where the deceased lay upon the ground, and turned the body over.[12]

It was a cloudless night, bright moon light and electric lights, and none of the fifteen witnesses saw or claimed to have seen any act of Frank W. that would even indicate the use of the knife upon the fallen body of John C., with the exception of John Zeilinski. And Zeilinski, in his testimony on his fight with John C., was without corroboration and was contradicted by every circumstance and the whole surroundings.[13]

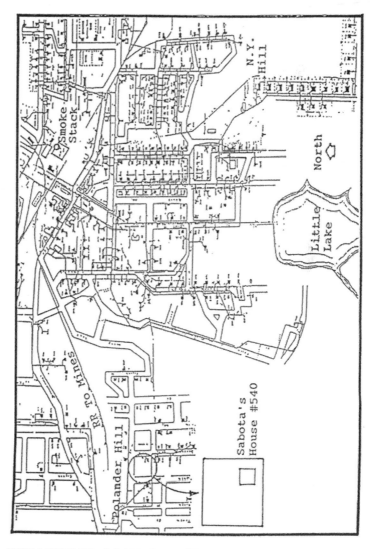

THE MURDER OCCURRED NEAR SABOTA'S HOUSE #540

The State, in zealously seeking a conviction, ignored the law, or perhaps knowing that Frank W.'s legal counsel was weak, used questionable ethics. For example, other than the testimony of John Zeilinski, who turned State's witness, who started the fight, and who fought the deceased, John C., there was no testimony that Frank W. had committed any offense. And Zeilinski's testimony was not corroborated, but was contradicted by all witnesses![14]

It was a strange twist when John Zeilinski, an accomplice in the fight with John C., was permitted to turn State's witness, but the jury was never told he was an accomplice![15] So, it came down to whom the jury believed, and Zeilinski was the only witness to claim Frank W. used his knife on the fallen body of John C. The testimony contracting Zeilinski was given by Walter Cukierski, but this was not admitted in Frank W.'s defense because Cukierski was under indictment for the same murder charge, and had not yet been tried![16] There was no official autopsy, and therefore, no description of the death instrument's blade length or width. But Dr. Dorsett did state that any ordinary pocket knife could have caused the fatal wound. Therefore, there was no proof that death resulted from Frank W.'s knife.[17]

The essential elements for First Degree Murder; expressed malice and premeditated intent, were not shown. The defendant, Frank W., was barely acquainted with the deceased, John C. The drunken brawl was instantaneous and unpremeditated, lasting but a few minutes, and Frank W.'s focus was on Joe Sikoski. And this battle was a separate and distinct affair from the fight in which John C. was killed.[18]

The court refused to allow Alford Clark, W.W. King and Robert Ivey to testify as to the defendant's honesty and good reputation; stating that the State had not put in issue Defendant's reputation for veracity. But this ruling was contrary to law; i.e., "... where material, the defendant may place in issue his general reputation upon any proposition that may be a defense in his support." Thus, "...it was left as a matter of veracity between defendant Frank W. and John Zeilinski to be believed by the jury as to which of the two had sworn to the truth ..."[19] But Frank W.'s good character was never sworn to in this court, and unfortunately, the jury believed John Zeilinski.

At the time of the murder, Frank Wisnoski was married but living separately from his wife Agnes. His wife was granted a divorce and custody of four children on December 4, 1918, seventeen months after Frank W. was pardoned. In the Divorce Petition, the wife claimed the defendant "...wilfully deserted and abandoned her on or about the 8th day of July 1917, when he was pardoned..."[20] And, that she had "...worked and earned her own living for the past thirteen years..."[21] Thus, a troubled marriage, even before the murder conviction, was dissolved after Frank W.'s incarceration and pardon.

Frank W. married a second time in 1930. He died in Yuba City, California in 1955.

In 1994 Frank W.'s youngest sister recalled the trial and "... that one of the three men who was fighting with the victim later committed suicide, and when his wife was on her death bed she confessed that her husband was the one who did the stabbing. This must have been when Frank received his pardon..."[22]

Although Frank's sister could not recall this man's name, from what is known now, it can be alleged this man was John Zeilinski. Zeilinski turned State's witness, probably to conceal his guilt, and he was the only one to testify that Frank W. was the guilty one. And testimony was that Zeilinski started the fight and fought with the victim, John Czerwinski. Zeilinski's suicide was probably from a tortured conscience.

Frank Wisnoski's fight was not with the victim, but Frank became a secondary victim on this "Green Sunday;" a day of peace and joy.

A MURDER IN THURBER NOTES

1. Halina Jarka Conversation, Fort Worth, TX, January 1996.

2. Mildred Shirley and Jean Mansell, "Erath County Deaths Reported," Abilene Reporter-News (Date unknown, copy in writer's collection).

3. Stephenville Empire, Stephenville, TX, May 31, 1912.

4. Ibid, June 7, 1912.

5. Assignments of Error, District Court of Erath County, TX, No. 3784, State of Texas v. Frank Wisnoski, Stephenville, TX, June Term 1912.

6. Criminal Court Minutes No. 3784, Vol. F, p. 138, District Court, Stephenville, TX, Aug 8, 1912.

7. Stephenville Empire, June 18, 1912.

8. Pardons No 15102, Gov. James E. Ferguson, Texas State Archives, Austin, TX, July 6, 1917.

9. Assignments of Error, Seventh Assignment, p. 7. Also 1910 Census for Sabota's House Number.

10. Ibid, Sixth Assignment, p. 6.

11. Citizenship Papers for Frank Wisnoski, Twin Falls, Idaho, Nov 18, 1939.

12. Assignments of Error, Ninth Assignment, p. 8.

13. Ibid, p. 8.

14. Ibid, Sixth Assignment, p. 6.

15. Ibid, Ninth Assignment, p. 8.

16. Ibid.

17. Ibid, First Assignment, p. 1.

18. Ibid, Third Assignment, p. 3.

19. Divorce Petition, Agnes Wisnoski, Milwaukee County, WI, par. 11, Dec 4 1918.

20. Ibid, Par 12.

21. Ltr from Betty Schilling, Frank W.'s granddaughter, 5 May 1994.

22. Ibid.

THE MYSTERY OF THURBER'S NEWCASTLE MINE

In thirty-eight years of coaling operations, from 1888 to 1926, the Texas and Pacific Coal Company acquired 24,000 acres of coal lands in Palo Pinto and Eastland counties. There are detailed descriptions for each of the company's sixteen mines.[1] Yet another mine, the Newcastle Mine, was located on company property just a mile south of #1 Mine, but unaccountably, this mine has not been documented in company archives or described in other literature.

Attention was focused on Newcastle Mine as recently as 1978 because its 16 to 24-foot coal depth was suitable for strip mining. Prior to strip mining, an archaeological study concluded: "When it (Newcastle) was closed is unknown as is who owned and operated it."[2] "Although the Newcastle Mine has been identified, it has been difficult to locate informants or documentation about the mine's history. ...it is recommended that the Newcastle Mine be nominated to the National Register of Historic places so that its importance can be recognized on a local as well as national basis."[3]

The Second Annual Report for the Geological Survey of Texas, 1890, shows that Mine #1 and Newcastle Mine were on the same rail Spur which connected to the E-W main line of the Texas and Pacific Railroad. This report stated: "For some reason the mine (Newcastle) was not running at the time of my last visit, but the suspension was only temporarily; yet it prevented me from getting the facts as fully as I wished in regard to their operations...The property has recently changed hands, and the present owners propose to develop their property to its fullest capacity."[4] But the "present owners" and the history of the mine have remained unknown until recently when several documents were linked together to show that Newcastle Mine originated with brothers William Whipple and Harvey E. Johnson. Newcastle Mine was on Section 24, owned by G.M. Allen and the Pickelsimer brothers, and transactions on this land show that the Johnsons purchased this tract in April 1887.[5]

Previously, the Johnsons began the first coal mine in Thurber in the fall of 1886, and this mining venture was incorporated as the "Johnson Coal Mining Co."[6]

On 23 November 1887, the Johnsons formed another company, the Palo Pinto Coal Mining Company, with J. W. Scheuber and J.G. Watkins. Since the Johnsons' first venture, the "Johnson Coal Mining Co." was badly underfinanced and in trouble,[7] the Johnsons probably brought in Scheuber and Watkins to bolster financing for their second mining venture, the Newcastle Mine. The proposed $600,000 capital stock of the P. P. C. M. Co. was divided evenly between the two Johnsons and the two other participants.[8] On 26 November 1887 there were two $10,000 promissory notes from the four partners to Sam Hunter, trustee for Horton Walker, a Canadian.[9] Although the P. P. C. M. Co. is not mentioned in this document, this money might have been used to develop Newcastle Mine, which was called "Shaft # 2" in legal documents.[10] Dumble's 1890 Survey is the first reference to this mine as "Newcastle Mine."[11] The origin of the name "Newcastle" is not known, perhaps after the mines in Newcastle, Wales. The name "Palo Pinto Coal Mining Co." was misleading, because the coal was mined in Erath County; not in Palo Pinto County.

The Johnson brothers came to Texas in 1879 under a legal cloud seeking escape from one hundred creditors and $18,000. in debts, from a failed merchandise business in Ionia, Michigan.[12] But the Johnsons were crafty in caching enough merchandise and money to open a merchandise, feed and cedar post business in southern Palo Pinto County, Texas on the Texas and Pacific RR line at Strawn, and profits from this venture enabled the Johnson brothers to become coal operators. But on 28 January 1888, Harvey E. Johnson died, leaving everything to his brother W.W. Johnson.

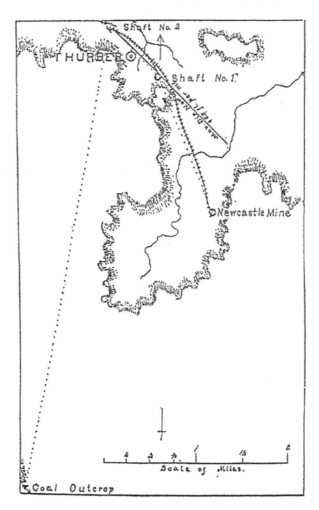

THURBER AND THE NEWCASTLE MINE IN ERATH COUNTY
Taken from the Second Annual Report of the
Geological Survey of Texas, 1890 by E. T. Dumble, Plate XI

On 24 February 1888, Allen and wife conveyed to Palo Pinto Coal Mining Co. 640 acres in Section 21.[13] And at this time the T & P RR continued its cooperation with the Johnsons by extending the rail spur one mile south from Johnson's #1 Mine to the Palo Pinto Co. Newcastle Mine.[14]

In March 1888 Johnson received a letter from T & P RR which threatened to remove the rail spur unless the quality and quantity of coal improved.[15] The letter might have served to pressure Johnson to sell the Johnson Coal Mining Co. (Mine Shaft #1) to R.D. Hunter but it might also have truthfully referred to the quality of coal at Newcastle because the shallow depth (16' to 24') of Newcastle coal evidently affected the quality. "Their shaft (Newcastle) ... was put down near the eastern edge of the outcrop, and the coal has been colored a little by the oxidation of the iron..."[16] On the other hand, an 1886 coal assay from the 65 feet-deep #1 Mine just one mile north of Newcastle, was most favorable.[17]

Bill Lollie, Superintendent of Strip Mining at Thurber in the 1980's, stated the coal near Newcastle had relatively low BTU's compared to other strip-mined coal at Thurber.[18] Therefore, the inferior coal at Newcastle might have justified the 1888 complaint from T & P RR. Inferior quality meant little demand for Newcastle coal, and Lollie's observation was that comparatively little coal was mined at Newcastle. "When we were strip-mining in the 1980's the main tunnel at Newcastle was uncovered. There were several coal cars, but we could only extract a few because of cave-in danger. There were several tunnels off the main shaft but these were not very large or deep, just about big enough for a coal car."[19] Indeed, the shallow coal depth would not have been conducive to the "advancing wall" mining method used in the deeper T & P Coal Co. Mines at Thurber. On 2 April 1888 the Palo Pinto Coal Mining Co. borrowed $50,000 from Central Trust Co. of New York and the agreement stated "...this company is in good standing and has no indebtedness either bonded or otherwise..."[20]

Some of this money may have been used to pay off the $20,000 promissory notes to Horton Walker, because on 5 April 1888, Johnson, Scheuber and Watkins paid this debt, said notes two months overdue at this time.[21]

This indenture with Central Trust was signed by J.G. Watkins, Secretary, and Wm. J. Provines, President of Palo Pinto Coal Mining Co. Johnson's name does not appear on this document, and it was about this time when R.D. Hunter began serious negotiations with W.W. Johnson to purchase the Johnson Coal Mining Co. (Mine Shaft #1). Hunter had previously inspected Mine #1 in August 1887 and was very favorably impressed with the coal property.[22] Hunter knew the Johnson Coal Mining Co. was under-financed and deeply in debt[23] and he probably used this to his advantage in securing Johnson's coal lands. Johnson was incensed at Hunter's penurious offer but because of his financial situation he had to accept Hunter's terms and the sale was completed in November 1888. But Johnson did manage to hold back the Newcastle Mine and three sections of land, perhaps to "get back" at Hunter and his T & P Coal Co. for taking advantage of him, or, Johnson might have needed the Newcastle Mine to further another financial scheme. But certainly, the shallow Coal depth (16' to 24') at Newcastle was a decided advantage in labor and equipment costs over the 65-foot depth at Mine #1. But the Newcastle Mine produced more litigation than coal.

William W. Johnson has been recognized as "An Enterprising Man"[24] and Newcastle was another example of Johnson's "wheeling and dealing" which often went beyond "enterprising" and kept him in litigation most of his life.[25] Indeed, the courts had to finally resolve the sale of the Johnson Coal Mining Co. to R.D. Hunter.[26]

As an illustration of his "enterprising" nature, in a fifteen-year period following the sale of his coal interests to Hunter in November

1888, W.W. Johnson was involved in twenty various business ventures, including lumber, railroads, banking, livery stable, gas company, cattle, silver, copper, agate, and galena mines, oil, a school and seven different coal endeavors in the area: Palo Pinto Coal Mining Co., Weatherford Coal Co., American Coal Co., Central Coal Co., Standard Coal Co., a royalty mineral owner in some coal land, and owner of Mount Marion Coal Co.[27] Johnson was not keen for the mundane day-to-day operation of a business; his expertise was in developing and promoting a business scheme.

Hunter's T and P Coal Co. expanded its coal operations by opening Mine #2 in 1889 and Mine #3 in 1891. The T & P RR probably refused to buy the inferior Newcastle coal and this would have aided Hunter in "freezing out" the Palo Pinto Coal Mining Co. and its Newcastle Mine. By 12 September 1890, the Newcastle Mine was defunct and the assets of the company were seized by Sheriff Shands and sold for $125 to H.C. Burlew of Dallas on 7 October 1890,[28] a far disparity from the $600,000 Newcastle stock proposal a few years earlier!

For $1,000, H.C. Burlew, on 17 September 1891, conveyed to John Hardie the Newcastle Mine and lands of the Palo Pinto Mining Co. and "...all the mining tools, tracks for railway and coal car, iron implements, machinery, railroad track scales..."[29]

But legal problems continued. In October 1896 the estate of one Susan Spofford, deceased, prevailed in a lawsuit against W.E. Kay, J.G. Watkins, Horton Walker and others involved with the Newcastle Mine. In this case, 486 acres of Newcastle land was awarded the Spofford estate.[30]

It appeared that John Hardie had bought the Newcastle Mine and lands in 1891. But records show that on 7 December 1900 he paid $75. to the City National Bank of Fort Worth, John Peter Smith, Receiver, for a 9/50th (9 bonds) part of land sections #24, #21 and #4, which were the three land sections involving Newcastle Mine.[31]

Finally, Texas and Pacific Coal Co. whose 22,000 acres entirely surrounded the 1,920 acres of Newcastle, began acquiring the Newcastle land. On 7 February 1901 the Company paid the Spofford Estate $1,458 for 486 acres of Newcastle land.[32] Eventually the company would acquire all three sections of this land, which brought their land total to about 24,000 acres.

But Texas and Pacific Coal Co. never mined any coal at Newcastle; therefore, Newcastle Mine operations have never been documented in Company records.

MYSTERY OF THURBER'S NEWCASTLE MINE NOTES

1. S. M. Greenidge, "Report on Coal Reserves of Texas Pacific Coal and Oil Company in Eastland, Erath, Palo Pinto and Parker Counties, Texas," Dallas: Texas Pacific Oil Co., 1953.

2. S. Alan Skinner, "Archaeology of the Thurber Coal Lease," Southern Methodist University Archaeology Research Program, 1978, p. 13.

3. Ibid. pp. 40, 41.

4. E. T. Dumble, "Second Annual Report of the Geological Survey of Texas, 1890," "Austin: State Printing Office, P. 532."

5. Erath County Clerk Records, Stephenville, TX: Book Y, p. 311.

6. Robert William Spoede, "William Whipple Johnson: An Enterprising Man," Abilene: Master's Thesis, Hardin Simmons Univ., July 1968, p. 49.

7. Ibid. p. 60.

8. Ibid. p. 54.

9. Erath County, Book E, p. 22.

10. Ibid.

11. Dumble, p. 531.

12. Spoede, p. 15.

13. Erath County, Book X, p. 402.

14. Spoede, p. 54.

15. Ibid. p. 62.

16. Dumble, p. 532.

17. Spoede, p. 47.

18. Bill Lollie, Willow Park, TX: Interview August 1994.

19. Ibid.

20. Erath County, Book E, p. 121.

21. Erath County, Vol. 28, p. 132.

22. Spoede, p. 65.

23. Ibid. P. 61.

24. Spoede, Title of Master's Thesis.

25. Ibid. pp. 35, 40, 70, 79, 85, 104, 109, 113, 131 etc.

26. Leo S. Bielinski, The Back Road to Thurber, Baird, TX: Joy Presswork Collection, 1993, p. 69.

27. Ibid. pp. 155-157.

28. Erath County, Vol. 30, p. 441.

29. Erath County, Vol. 36, p. 448.

30. Erath County, Vol. 53, p. 427.

31. Erath County, Vol. 65, p. 279.

32. Erath County, Vol. 74, p. 130.

SETTING THE RECORD STRAIGHT

The literature on Thurber is quite extensive with six books,[i] several theses, dozens of periodical articles, hundreds of newspaper reports and one DVD which has been shown several times on national TV. Thurber is indeed a fantastic read. In its time a modern city of several thousand, today Thurber is a ghost town traversed each day by 13,200 vehicles traveling I-20.[1]

Thurber's Texas and Pacific Coal Co. helped open up the Southwest by providing a dependable fuel supply for the railroads from 1888 to 1926. In 1917 this Thurber-based Company, under the legendary W.K. Gordon, brought in the Ranger Oil Field ("The Oil Field that won WWI")[2] and from this discovery oil exploration spread throughout West Texas. This was propitious because America began to travel about this time and petroleum products were needed for cars and airplanes. And millions of Thurber Bricks paved the streets and highways.

The 1903 Thurber Miners' Strike was a consequential milestone for the Labor Movement in this region. Sixteen different nationalities populated Thurber; mostly Italian and Polish immigrants. Thurber was a modern community and had its own electrical plant in 1895. It was the first totally unionized community in the world, and a company town with no municipal government, no unemployment, no taxes and virtually no crime.

With so many interesting facets and so much written matter for reference, it is understandable that Thurber is an appealing subject

---

[i] Fire in a Hole!, Hardman; Life of the Texas Pacific Coal & Oil Co., Studdard; A Way of Work and Way of Life: Coal Mining in Thurber, Texas, Rhinehart; Thurber, Texas, Spratt; The Back Road to Thurber, Bielinski; Black Diamonds! Black Gold!: the Saga of Texas Pacific Coal and Oil Company, Woodard.

for writers at all levels. But unfortunately, some writers quote misleading references which have but *prima facie* plausibility, or they interpret material to fit their own misconceptions. And a false picture of Thurber emerges where totally false information is referenced and quoted time and again. For example, a purported picture of Thurber's "Horseshoe Bar" in the Snake Saloon is frequently seen in the literature. But it is quite obvious that this is not a horseshoe-shaped bar, nor *the* "Horseshoe Bar" which was in Thurber's downtown Snake Saloon. This picture is that of the long ("as long as two train cars")[3] straight bar in the second Snake Saloon just inside Palo Pinto County. Some writer mislabeled the unmistakably straight bar, and others blindly accepted it and referenced it!

This writer's generation is the last generation with a direct link to Thurber, and having lived in the shadow of Thurber for eighty-five years, there is a strong urge to point out misconceptions on Thurber, for soon there will be no one left to correct the misstatements. The writer's family has been a part of the Thurber locale for over one hundred years, Grandfather Piotr Wasieleski migrating from Sierpc, Poland to Thurber in 1890 and working in the mines thirty-one years. The writer's mother was born in Thurber and in her ninety years never lived farther than two miles from Thurber. The writer has prowled over much of Thurber and some of the mine locations.

Descendants of Thurber Poles are annoyed when some writers misinterpret census data to omit Poles from Thurber's population. In the census, when Country of Origin is "Russia-Poland," "Germany-Poland" or "Austria-Poland," the erroneous assumption is that the person was Russian, German or Austrian, respectively; therefore, according to such misinterpretation, there were no Poles in Thurber. Despite these countries having occupied Poland from 1795-1918, Poles have never lost ethnic identity.

Two of the most authoritative and informative books on Thurber are Studdard's Life of the T P Coal & Oil Co. and Hardman's Fire in a Hole! Studdard and Hardman both lived and worked in Thurber and had firsthand knowledge of people and events. Although Thurber offers many aspects for research and study, many writers have never visited Thurber, and much written material does not involve original research but is merely a rehash of the same old story with the same old references. Academics require careful references, but the thinking is that more references (rather than reliability of references) indicate the subject matter has been thoroughly researched.

One of the most widely-disseminated Thurber misconceptions is totally misleading when it implies there was a "jumble of houses with little thought to planning or layout of residential houses." And this notion had been referenced and twisted around until a 20 Nov 1996 magazine story on Thurber provoked the following response:

Editor
Magazine
Fort Worth, Texas

RE: THURBER LOST 20 Nov 1996

Here's a Thurber map, show me "...a hodgepodge of buildings. There tenements looked as though they had fallen out of the sky with no regard for arrangement." Your writer is like many writers who seize an isolated incident or opinion on Thurber, add their own twist, are published, and the misinformation on Thurber spreads. Thurber General Manager W. K. Gordon was a surveyor and exceedingly neat and precise in all his planning and work.

The Thurber Cemetery Association is not aware that "One of the main concerns today is protecting Thurber Cemetery

from vandals." **Strange that a picture of my family plot appears above this caption.**

My grandfather, Piotr Wasieleski, came from Poland to Thurber in 1890. My family has been a part of the Thurber locale for over 100 years. Thurber's Poles were Catholic. I've never heard of a "Polish Bar Mitzvah."

If your writer had looked south across I-20, he would have seen the other half of Thurber; a miner's house, the 100-year-old St. Barbara's Church, a train car, bocci ball courts, New York Hill etc.

Before you go off "half-cocked" again, check with the Thurber Historical Association which was organized in 1937.

Sincerely,
Leo S. Bielinski Ph.D.

Sometimes it appears as if all references on Thurber were fed into a computer, and when a reference was needed, it was pulled off the computer with but little thought to applicability or source. For example, an Ivy League School study is quoted that Thurber was a "Sicilian Community." Had the author studied demographics or talked to remaining descendants of Thurber's Italians it would have been abundantly clear that Thurber's foreign-born were predominantly northern Italian. If Thurber were a Sicilian Community, Thurber's Italian Hill should have been named "Sicilian Hill."

Recruitment of Eastern Europeans to Thurber was effectively accomplished by written word, and a letter and "passage money" from a Thurber relative was inducement to migrate. It was not uncommon to find several members of one family from the "Old

Country" working in Thurber: brothers, uncles, nephews, fathers and sons and cousins. Most Italians came from northern Italy such as the Venice, Bologna and Turin regions and villages like Modena, Costello, Piva Pelligo, Pomonti, Pumentizzi, Gruppo, Frignana, Riolunato, Pievepelago, Veneto, Treviso d'Asolo, and Zenone.[4] It is both fortunate and unfortunate that early writers sought out only one source for mining and union activities: fortunate, in that there is a written record of some of these events and unfortunate, in that this gives an over-referenced and one-sided view.

In Mingus and Strawn in the 1930s and 1940s, there were dozens of early Thurber miners, including John Obel, John Piacentini, Joe Daskevich, Gigi Biondini, Luigi Solignani, Frank Lenzini, John Zinanni, etc. who had lived and worked in Thurber. Perhaps a personal, written account was not likely, but an oral interview was possible. Although most of these opportunities were missed, Lawrence Santi, a Local Union official (UMW, the "Italian" Local #2753), and executive board member for Texas in UMW District 21 (Texas, Oklahoma and Arkansas) was finally interviewed in 1974.[5]

Jake Galik would have provided interesting information first, from an immigrant perspective since he was a Polish miner. And he was one of the fourteen signers of the 1903 union demands which preceded the historic Miners Strike.[6] "Jack Garlic" was the name by which newspapers called Jake Galik. These were the 14 men who were the union activists and who had their "necks stuck out" during the 1903 strike.[ii] These early Thurber miners talked of their experiences to family and friends, but nothing was ever written down.

[ii] J. A. Osborn, J. W. Lloyd, John Gaines, Will Smith, W. W. Oliver, Jake Galik, Konrad Wahard, Gior Guiseppe, Peter Grosso, John Rolando, F. F. Versracten, Anton Bertrom, Paul Piffer, Joseph Rendzoner.

Some of the Thurber literature has an absurd conclusion of the existence of a "low-rental area" on Park Row near the baseball park (as if one could shop around and rent a house in an area of choice).

Also, it was claimed that this was a desirable neighborhood because of its greater distance from the mines. The standard rent for all Thurber box-type housing (Park Row included) was $6 a month for a three-room house.[7] And $2 more for an extra bedroom.

From 1894 to 1911 "distance from mines" could not be a factor in desirable living areas because all operating mines were well west of Thurber's residential areas, and miners rode a train several miles to work. The coal vein extended in a westerly direction, and distance to mines caused General Manager W.K. Gordon to think about establishing another town nearer the mines.[8] If indeed, "distance from mines" was a desirable factor in living conditions, there was also an undesirable feature for downtown: with a prevailing south wind, downtown Thurber was often clouded with dense black coal smoke from the downtown power house and brickyard chimneys.

Statements like, "...the mine dump, the shale dump and the railroad spur always dominated the scene..." and "...most of the houses sat on rocky soil that never produced greenery," conjure a dead, dreary, ugly landscape. But this is not right, for most Thurber homes were in the fertile valley formed by the five hills of Thurber, and this soil would grow most anything with normal rainfall. Lawns were an unnecessary luxury for most working folks, but roses, vines, grape arbors and shrubs were very much in evidence.[9]

**LOOKING NORTHWEST TOWARD DOWNTOWN THURBER
FROM ATOP BRICKYARD HILL. BRICKYARD AND
BRICKYARD SMOKE STACK IN FOREGROUND**

When Thurber was being demolished in the early 1930s, dozens of Thurber Junction/Mingus people dug up Thurber greenery for transplanting.[10] Today, Thurber's landscape still belies the misconception "rocky soil---no greenery," because former residential areas now abound in wheat and oats for grazing goats and cattle. In the Thurber Cemetery on top of Graveyard Hill there are irises and a solid carpet of Indian Paintbrush and Indian Blanket in spring, which in summer give way to Phlox and Siderwort.

The mine dumps never dominated any residential view because Mines #2, #3 and # 4, which were in the residential areas, were short-lived and abandoned by 1894.[11] The mine tailings from these mines were used to extend the rail bed westward. The folks living on Polander and Italian Hills had a good view of the city below; indeed, a view not obstructed or "dominated" by mine dumps or rail spur.

It has been implied that social standing was a function of how close one lived to downtown Thurber. Therefore, the folks living on

Italian and Polander Hill, a quarter-mile to the west, were a lower level of society. As the city expanded westward, and the foreign-born population increased, Italians and Poles tended to group on the Hill, but there were still many Italians and Poles living below the Hill, near downtown, and these were dubbed the "Downhill Gang."[12] The houses on the Hill were not the "least expensive" and most rundown because these houses were built later than the houses nearer downtown. The African-Americans lived close to downtown Thurber, at the bottom of New York Hill, but that did not give them a higher social standing than the New England oil people on NY Hill. If there were social distinctions, it was among the white collar workers who lived on "Silk Stocking Row" (Marston Avenue) or the oil people on New York Hill, for their parties, visitors, marriages, births and deaths were reported in the "Thurber Journal," while events of the foreign-born went unreported. The majority of Thurberites did the same work (mining and brick-making), resided in similar houses in all parts of Thurber, shopped the same facilities, attended the same operas, drank in the same saloon and worshiped in the same churches. Social distinction was not a function of how far one lived from a mine, but rather if one were a blue collar or white collar worker.

A New York study is referenced that Italian immigrants in particular, after making some money in America, intended to return to their homeland. And this "...reduced Americanization and naturalization to secondary considerations." But this generalization should not be applied to Thurber Italians, for what was true in New York did not necessarily apply to Thurber. It is true that some Thurber Italians did go back to Italy, but the majority was here to stay, particularly those with families. And many bought land and homes in adjacent Thurber Junction, while others moved on to other locations in America. Accordingly, they wanted to be good Americans, to adopt American ways and to not stand out for ridicule as "foreigners." Thurber Italians believed their Americanization would be helped by joining fraternal lodges such as the Odd Fellows, Red Men or Knights of Pythias and this they did in large numbers.[13] The "Thurber Diaspora" is throughout the United States and perhaps two hundred thousand people can trace their origins in America to Thurber.

Similarly, there is the unsubstantiated conclusion that Thurber immigrants made "little effort to learn English." Many Thurber immigrants were already bilingual in European languages. Italian-born miner Tony Gardetto, at the 1903 Rocky Creek union meeting, translated spoken English into Italian, French and Spanish.[14] The 1920 Thurber Census records indicate that most foreign-born did not read or write English, but this does not mean they could not *speak* "passable" English, for many certainly conducted successful businesses and bootlegging operations in nearby Thurber Junction. Thurber Census records show that every school-age, American-born child of foreign-born parents could read and write English. This writer attended school with dozens of children of foreign-born parents and the preceding statement is definitely true. Parents wanted their offspring to be "good Americans."[15]

While Thurber's ethnic groups tended to cluster, they did not continue to dress in their "colorful native costumes," as some writers think; to do so would invite derision. And only American-style suits and dresses and dry goods were available in company stores.

The generally accepted figure for the peak population of Thurber has been 10,000. But the 1910 Census count is 3,805 and the 1920 count is 3,596. Maximum coal production was in 1915, and the population most likely peaked at this time. Probably 5,000 would be a more realistic figure. Some writers may get differing figures because they may count *all* residents in Precinct #7, rather than just those in "Thurbertown." In 1920 there were 752 numbered houses in Thurber, and if one did not live in a numbered Thurber house, he should not be counted as a resident of Thurber.

The immigrants came to Thurber to escape harsh social/economic conditions in their place of origin. They were grateful for their new home in America, and for work in the Thurber coal mines, and that's what they did in Thurber. It was hard work, but it was an opportunity which was lacking in the "Old Country," and they seized the opportunity. Apparently, some writers are not aware of this when they make inane, obvious, superficial statements such as "...country of origin (or ethnicity) and related language capabilities constituted important determinants of occupation, housing patterns, and social/economic positions in community." But many Thurber miners were American-born and literate in the English language. And they worked alongside the foreign-born miners and were paid the same scale and lived in the same type houses.

The 1920 Thurber Census showed 164 white collar workers and 739 blue collar workers. After the Ranger Oil Boom in 1917, most unmarried white collar workers lived in Marston Hall, a Methodist boarding house on Thurber's Plaza. Most married white collar workers lived in a few dozen small brick homes on Marston Street or in 34 newer homes (built after 1917) on New York Hill. The remaining several hundred houses in Thurber were of box-type construction and were common in all sections of Thurber. Contrary to some writers' statements, most Thurber houses were not of "shot gun" design but were "T" shaped, the kitchen being the stem of the "T." Others were "L" shaped.

There are statements that UMW John L. Lewis came to Thurber every two years at labor contract renewal time. Lawrence Santi, a Thurber union official, said Lewis never set foot in Thurber, and that he (Santi) should know.[16] Surely, there would have been many pictures of the renowned labor leader's Thurber visits. But there is only one picture of John L. Lewis meeting with T & P President Marston and W.K. Gordon and this was taken at the "Worth Hotel, Fort Worth, Texas, in September 1903."[17] Sometimes this picture is shown without this caption, hence an incorrect assumption is made that the picture was taken in Thurber. The only other identified person in this picture is the third man from the right, Jacob Galik, a Polish miner and one of the fourteen signers of the union demands which preceded the 1903 strike. Thurber was totally unionized, and any Thurber visit by such a prominent labor official would have been very disruptive.

One writer refers to an Erath County School Superintendent's Record 1890-1891, which asserts "White children attended the Thurber School, black children attended the Hunter School..." But the Hunter Academy, a Catholic School named after the Company President R.D. Hunter, did not open until 1894. With 400 students, it was staffed by the Sisters of Incarnate Word, and W.K. Gordon's children and Catholic as well as many non-Catholic children attended this academy. The academy was open to all ethnic groups, but Raymond Bridier, who attended this school, never saw a black student in attendance.[18] Thurber did have a small, separate black school which was located in the black housing section at the base of New York Hill. There was also a kindergarten (next to House #641) on Italian Hill which was a big help for very busy Italian mothers who had boarders in their homestead.

Rocky Creek Bridge, about midway between Thurber and Lyra (near Strawn) figures in misinformation about Thurber. As recounted in newspapers, an emotional, consequential union organizational meeting was held at this bridge on Thursday September 10, 1903. Despite the significance of this all-important meeting, at least four writers have inaccurately described the location of this meeting place, probably because they quoted inaccurate references.

Although Joe Fenoglio is seldom mentioned in Thurber literature, he played a very significant role in the 1903 Thurber Miners strike. The Italians were the majority work force whose support was needed by the UMW to ensure a successful strike. At great personal risk,

Fenoglio very effectively organized the Italian miners thereby resulting in a successful strike.

There is an 1889 reference which claimed that dual unionism was an "acute" problem in Thurber. But this cannot be true because by 1889 T & P President Hunter had quashed the Knights of Labor Union and Thurber was an absolute open shop for fourteen years (1889 to 1903). Before focusing on Thurber, the UMW (United Mine Workers) had control in most other parts of the country. For example, the UMW had established Locals in nearby Lyra and Strawn before organizing Thurber miners in 1903. In 1906 the Italian miners protested because they had the most union members in Thurber, but only Americans served as union officials, and these officials ignored the grievances and religious holidays of the Italians. To avoid friction the UMW granted another Local charter to the Italian miners (UMW Local No. 2753), and all immigrant miners joined this Local which became several times larger than the original Local. Thurber had two UMW Locals, and if this is what was meant by "dual Unionism," it did not happen until 1906.

W.K. Gordon brought Texas Pacific Coal and Oil Co. to prominence and great wealth with Thurber coal and Ranger oil. One author states that Gordon built himself a palace in Thurber, but this is both inaccurate and misleading. The company built and owned all buildings and Gordon's home was a typical structure befitting a General Manager.

One book on Thurber states that the 1903 Miner's Strike was a *Pyrrhic victory*. Not true, for the settling of this strike brought about many peaceful years and permitted Thurber to prosper. This successful strike was a tremendous boost for the labor movement in the Southwest; miners got better pay and the fence around Thurber came down.

When the railroads switched to oil, there was no way for the company to "regain its market for coal." The miners in 1921 did not ask for more money thus, a higher wage scale did not force the company out of the coal business. The focus was on oil, and the company had plenty in its nearby Ranger Oil Field. But the company had to keep some mines open to fulfill existing coal contracts. The miners did not strike. The company canceled its existing contract with the UMW and announced a reduction in wages. Take it or leave it. And this is a classic example of a "lockout" which Lawrence Santi and others always claimed despite the accepted misconception that the mines closed in 1921 because the miners struck.

There was no "third assault" (strike) in 1926, for there was no union organization. The mines from 1921 to 1926 were operated with scab labor. The company had completed its coal contracts and closed the mines. The coal needed for industry was provided now by the nearby Strawn and Lyra mines (no connection to T P C & O Co).

There have been contradictory claims as to the first secretary of the Thurber UMW Local. In 1986 the author donated the original Thurber UMW Charter to University of Texas at Arlington Archives. The first secretary was William McKinnon.

The overly referenced source on Thurber union activities is unreasonably boastful when he asserts, "I know of no one living at this time (1940) who spent so much time in the active service of the union as myself for the period stated."(1884 – 1921) The fact is this person was in company management from 1888 to 1921 as weigh master, pit boss and mine superintendent. Lawrence Santi, Board Member of District UMW Union 21 and an official of Thurber UMW Local #2753, said that when this person accepted management he could not belong to the union.[19] Thus, the "active service" was more as an observer, and hence a second-hand source.

Although errors in Thurber history are inevitable, the problem is that such misinformation will be referenced and perhaps twisted farther and eventually the serious researcher might see Thurber literature which bears little resemblance to the true Thurber.

SETTING THE RECORD STRAIGHT NOTES

1. TXDOT (Texas Dept. Of Transportation), 1993 Survey, Gordon, TX office.

2. Sign on I-20 between Ranger Hill and Ranger, TX, 1992.

3. Willie M. Floyd, "Thurber, Texas, an Abandoned Coal Field Town," Dallas: Master's Thesis, Southern Methodist University, June 1939, p. 71.

4. Aldo J. Crovetti, Ltr. 24 March 1995, Lake Forest, IL. Ed Bernardi Ltr., 26 Jan 1995, Naples, FL. (Author's personal files).

5. Lawrence Santi, Interview by George Green, U of TX at Arlington, 1974.

6. Dallas Morning News, 11 Sept 1903.

7. Weldon B. Hardman, Fire in a Hole!, Gordon, TX: Thurber Historical Association, 1975, p. 102.

8. W. K. Gordon, Ltr. To Edgar L. Marston, Thurber, TX, Dec 10, 1906. (Copy in author's file).

9. Victor Lucadello, Manuscript on Thurber, Kenosha, WI, 1990. (Author's personal file). Hardman, p. 111.

10. In 1935 Thurber Junction families dug up Thurber flowers and shrubs for planting in their own yards in Thurber Junction.

11. S. M. Greenridge, "Texas and Pacific Coal and Oil Company Coal Production," Fort Worth, TX, 1953, p. 16.

12. Gino Solignani, Conversation, Mingus, TX, 1990.

13. Leo S. Bielinski, The Back Road to Thurber, Baird, TX: Joy Presswork Collection, 1993, p. 215.

14. Dallas Morning News, September 14, 1903.

15. Bielinski, p. 201.

16. Lawrence Santi, p. 35.

17. This picture is on display at New York Hill Restaurant, Thurber, TX.

18. Raymond Bridier, Conversation, Mansfield, TX, 1995.

19. Lawrence Santi, p. 33.

NEW YORK HILL'S PLACE IN THURBER HISTORY

Thurber's history could be divided into two overlapping eras: the Coal Era 1888-1921 and the Oil Era 1917-1933.

The Oil Era began when W.K. Gordon, Thurber's General Manager, brought in the Ranger Oil Field (The Oil Field that won WWI) in October 1917. This event changed Thurber's ambience and signaled the beginning of the end of Thurber, for now oil was in and coal was on its way out. In addition to being noted for its coal, brick, ethnic diversity and unionism, oil became the fifth major aspect of Thurber's being.

When the McClesky oil well blew in, Ranger boomed from a population of several hundred to 30,000, and housing and office space were practically nonexistent. Streets were knee-deep in mud. People slept in shifts in hotels. There was the usual run of humanity associated with an oil boom town, and the 1940 movie, "Boom Town," starring Clark Gable was inspired by this oil discovery.

There were few locals trained in oil field management, so Gordon's company, Texas & Pacific Coal Co. (T & P Coal Co.) brought in people from the New England states, mostly New Yorkers, to run its oil business. The company name was changed to T & P Coal and Oil Co. And from Thurber, these people managed the Ranger Oil field which was 15 miles west of Thurber. Some employees commuted to Ranger each day, or as their work required. While a drive of 15 miles by today's standards is nothing, but back then, a drive to Ranger could mean a challenging trip in climbing Ranger Hill, particularly in weather and if the car were a Model T Ford with only two forward gears.

131

These New Englanders were accustomed to a more sophisticated life style than the environment of a coal mining camp in north central Texas. They were used to indoor plumbing and homes more luxurious than the brick bungalows on Thurber's Marston Street which housed staff and managers of the coal company. And certainly, if they were to work in such an isolated place, they expected more than a miner's box-type house. The solution was to build thirty-four new houses on the hill east of Little Lake which was called "New York Hill" because many of the residents were from New York. A quarter-million dollars were spent on these houses, about $7,000. a house. This contrasts sharply with the cost of miners' houses built twenty years earlier at a cost of $150 – $200.

A brick sidewalk was built from downtown Thurber to the bottom of New York Hill. Brick steps climbed New York Hill and the sidewalk continued on to the houses. In 1992 the steps were restored, and portions of the original sidewalk are still visible both at the bottom and top of New York Hill.

An Episcopal Church was built on New York Hill, about where the restaurant is located today. The dirt road up New York Hill was called Church Street, because this street gave access to the Episcopal, the Baptist and the Negro Churches.

With the railroads changing to oil burning locomotives, the demand for coal was greatly reduced, and in 1921 the company canceled a contract with the UMW and closed the mines. However, there were still coal contracts to be filled, and the company reopened New #3 and #10 mines, but at a reduced output and with "scab" labor. Idled UMW miners were asked to vacate their Thurber houses and these deserted houses, with doors and windows removed, gave an eerie look to some sections of Thurber. The miners and their families moved into Tent City, which was located in an open field in Grant Town, just north of Thurber. They stayed in Tent City until they arranged for work in other parts of the country.

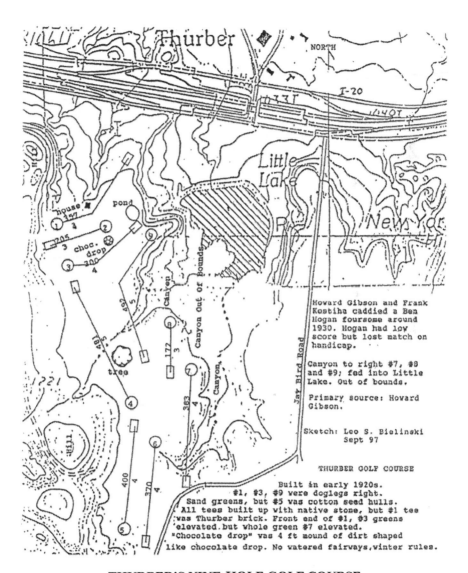

Howard Gibson and Frank Kostiha caddied a Ben Hogan foursome around 1930. Hogan had low score but lost match on handicap.

Canyon to right #7, #8 and #9; fed into Little Lake. Out of bounds.

Primary source: Howard Gibson.

Sketch: Leo S. Bielinski Sept 97

THURBER GOLF COURSE

Built in early 1920s. #1, #3, #9 were doglegs right. Sand greens, but #5 was cotton seed hulls. All tees built up with native stone, but #1 tee was Thurber brick. Front end of #1, #3 greens elevated but whole green #7 elevated. "Chocolate drop" was 4 ft mound of dirt shaped like chocolate drop. No watered fairways, winter rules.

THURBER'S NINE-HOLE GOLF COURSE
WAS SOUTH OF TODAY'S I-20 AND IS NO LONGER DISCERNABLE.

The New Englanders brought a different life style to Thurber which fit in with the times: The Roaring Twenties and Prohibition. There were formal dances and balls and parties at the private Thurber Club. Liquor could not be sold, but between dances the men would dash to individual lockers for a "snort." Lawrence Welk, Jan Garber and Jack Amelung were some of the big bands that performed.

A nine-hole golf course (sand greens) was built behind Thurber's Little Lake, and Ben Hogan played an exhibition match.

A bowling alley ("duck pins") was installed and fishing and hunting privileges at Thurber's Big Lake were granted. Living conditions were excellent and leisure time was enjoyable with plenty of activities and entertainment.

The company ran two "locals" a day (trains) from Thurber to Ranger. These trains carried pipe, tools, supplies and some commuting Thurberites. Other Thurberites made the fifteen-mile drive to the Ranger Oil Field by car, and this trip seems insignificant by today's mode. But in 1920 with muddy dirt/gravel roads, low powered cars, flat tires and blowouts and formidable Ranger Hill, a trip to Ranger could be an episode.

Ranger Hill lay several miles west of Thurber. It had a fairly steep gradient, rising about 200 feet in a mile. But by winding the road around the side of the hill, the climb was made less steep. However, with a poorly-tuned 20-40 HP car or truck, this was a task. And when Ranger Hill was conquered, there was a feeling of accomplishment. There was a roadside park with tables and benches at the top of the hill where one could pause or exult; cool down the car or make needed repairs. There is the claim that the west begins after Ranger Hill, because the hills diminish then and the land and trees become more uniform.

If the vehicle were a well-tuned, three forward speed; gear shift car, there was little difficulty, except perhaps for overheating. But most trucks with a load had to strain climbing the hill. However, in the days of the Ranger Oil Boom, Model T Fords were the most popular and affordable cars. A new Model T sold for $260. in 1925. From 1909 to 1927, 26,000,000 Fords were manufactured. The Model T developed 20 horsepower and had two speeds forward: low and high. The Model T had no equal on muddy roads, and with a "high center" and narrow 30 x 3-1/3 tires, it was almost impossible to stick. But climbing hills, like Ranger Hill, was a different story.

It was a common, but amusing sight to see Model T's backing up Ranger Hill. On the earlier Model T's, the gravity-fed gasoline tank was under the driver's seat. With a half-empty tank and a slight incline, the gasoline would not reach the carburetor. But this inconvenience could be overcome by backing up the hill, and this problem was corrected in later models by locating the gasoline tank under the dashboard. But there was another problem with this car which necessitated backing up Ranger Hill. The Model T Ford had three pedals: one for low speed, one for reverse and one for braking. To start forward, the low-speed pedal was pressed until some speed was attained, then a lever on the left side was pushed forward to put the car in high gear. The problem was that since the low-speed pedal was the most-used, its clutch band often wore out. When this happened, the only way to get up Ranger Hill was to use the reverse pedal and back up the hill.

Flat tires and tire blowouts were common because most roads were not paved and the tires were not very durable. There were no tubeless tires, no bias plies or steel belts, and there was no such thing as a tire guarantee because driving conditions were too unpredictable. All cars carried an air pump, a jack, tire-changing and flat-repairing tools and the "Monkey Grip" cold patch tube repair kit with glue for sticking the patch on the inner tube. The peril of automobile travel during the Ranger Oil Boom is best told by George Carter in a 1966 edition of the Pinto County Star:

"During the early part of the oil boom (1917) the jitney service in Thurber consisted of only two jitneys for hire. The jitneys were both Model T touring cars with curtains. One was owned by Ernest (Pee Wee) Keown, and the other was owned and operated by Henry Martin. Both of these cars were the 'crank off the magneto' kind with no battery. We didn't have pavements, and the roads in dry weather were full of chug holes, rocks, stumps, brush and high centers.

"In wet weather it was easy to get stuck, and if you had a flat tire it had to be fixed on the spot because there were no spare tires. We could get jitney service day or night, either Pee Wee or Henry were available most of the time. They made pretty good money running the jitneys.

"Late one Saturday I met Pee Wee at the Thurber Drug Store, and he told me that he was on his way to Ranger to pick up a driller and carry him to the Hohhertz Camp north of Strawn. He invited me to make the trip with him, and I agreed. It had been raining for two or three days, and everything was just floating in water. We got about halfway to Ranger, in what we called the 'Big Canyon' (on the side of Ranger Hill) and slid crossways in the road and stuck. It was pitch-dark by then and we only had an oil lantern for light. Pee Wee jacked up the front end of the jitney and then the back end. We carried logs, rocks and brush from the rattle snake infested hillside and finally got the Model T on solid ground once again. It took us three hours to get out of the mud hole.

"We finally made it into Ranger, picked up the driller and his suitcase and headed out for Hohhertz. About a mile past Strawn, the Ford suddenly stopped and Pee Wee said, 'George, we've got a flat tire.' It took us two hours to repair the tire. Pee Wee put a 'Monkey Grip' cold patch on the tube and started out again for Hohhertz. We finally unloaded the driller and his suitcase at a big tent camp in Hohhertz and started back to Thurber. We stuck in the mud again near the Davidson

Cemetery and once again shoveled mud and carried rocks and logs. We drove up to my Thurber residence at 3 A.M. Sunday morning. When I stepped out of the jitney, Pee Wee said, 'George, this is your last ride in my jitney, you're bad luck.' I had already decided that when we got stuck the first time. Later on we had a lot of fun recalling that trip."

Since Thurber was the headquarters for the growing T & P Coal and Oil Company, there were many visitors: oil operators, salesmen and business men. But suitable hotel accommodations were lacking, ever since the first-class Hotel Knox burned in 1907. Edgar L. Marston, President of the company, proposed a fine hotel on top of New York Hill, but this was never built. He wrote to a prominent Hotel man:

Van Noy Interstate Company,
Kansas City, Mo.   May 8, 1918

Dear Mr. Van Noy:

The Texas Pacific Coal and Oil Company has under consideration the construction of a hotel at Thurber. The hotel at Mingus on the line of the Texas & Pacific RR was burned down and the hotel at Thurber is almost a disgrace to the company.

Having had experience in hotel construction and management of hotels, I wonder if you would give me the benefit of your knowledge and experience by advising me the character of the hotel we should erect in Thurber. I do not know whether you have visited our little town, but now that we are the center of the oil operations, every day oil operators are visiting Thurber, and we should have suitable accommodations for them.

I have a beautiful site about six tenths of a mile from town and while the hotel should face the town which would be north, the cool side of the hotel is to the south. None of the officers of the company agree with me as to locating this hotel on the hill, as it is far for the traveling public and the employees of the company, but this does not influence me at all: for the reason that all visitors to Thurber come in automobiles, and second it would do the boys good to walk a half mile for their lunch, or after they are through at the office.

I have in mind a building of forty rooms with a general sitting room and a large dining room on the first floor.

It may be that the matter might become interesting to the Van Noy Company, if the Coal Company would guarantee any deficit up to $200. a month in operation.

**Yours Very Truly,
Edgar L. Marston, President**

In 1926 the coal mines permanently closed. The miner's houses were sold and moved off. In 1933 the Company moved its headquarters to Fort Worth. The fine houses on New York Hill, which each cost several thousand dollars to build, were sold for $250. and moved elsewhere. And some of these New York Hill houses are still being lived in today. New York Hill was barren again after only sixteen years as one of Thurber's focal points.

Today, a restaurant is located about where the Episcopal Church stood. The most often asked visitor's question is, "What's the gray castle farther up the hill?" The castle was not a part of Thurber but is a luxurious hunting lodge with a magnificent view of "Pickel Simon Valley" (Pickelsimmer) where mules and donkeys were rewarded with retirement after their work in the coal mines.

THE SEARCH FOR HARVEY
JOHNSON'S GRAVE

13 May 1989

To: Chamber of Commerce
Ionia, Michigan 48846

Tell me how I could find out if Harvey E. Johnson is buried in Ionia.

The Johnson brothers, W. W. and Harvey, came to Texas from Ionia in 1878 and started the coal industry at Thurber, Texas. Harvey died in January 1888, but because of debts in Ionia, W. W. was advised not to ship the body there for burial. However, Harvey's grave is not listed in the graves registry of Palo Pinto County, Texas. The Johnson family (father's name Ethan) remained in Michigan during the brothers' endeavors in Texas. W. W.'s grave, wife and two children's graves are on the Johnson Ranch north of Gordon, Texas. I have a feeling Harvey was buried in Ionia.

Cordially,
Leo S. Bielinski

From: IONIA AREA CHAMBER OF COMMERCE
May 16, 1989

Dear Mr. Bielinski,

139

The Ionia County Courthouse does not have records for cemeteries but does have records on births and marriage licenses, also people who died in Ionia County.

The addresses of the other two resources (Ionia Public Library and Ionia County Clerk) are listed on your original letter. Good luck in your search.

Sincerely,
Executive Director

A few years later, and after inquiries with no responses from two Ionia, Michigan Funeral Homes, a letter was written to the Public Library.

8 August 1994
Ionia Public Library
126 E. Main
Ionia, Michigan 48846

Does your library have Cemetery Tombstone Inscriptions for Ionia Cemeteries?

I'm trying to find out if Harvey E. Johnson is buried in Ionia. He was the son of Ethan S. and Jane B. Johnson. There were three girls and four boys. The two middle brothers were inmates of insane asylums. Two sisters married and remained in Ionia; one moved to California. The mother, Jane B., died in California in December 1902. The father, Ethan S., died in Ionia in 1883.

The first and third-born brothers, William W. and Harvey E., respectively, came to Texas from Ionia in 1878 and started the Texas Coal Industry at Thurber, Texas (ghost town today). Harvey died in January 1888, but because they were heavily indebted in Ionia because of a failed business, W. W. was advised not to ship the body back there for burial. But Harvey's grave is not listed in any of the counties around Thurber, Texas. W. W. was wealthy, and the two brothers were very close. So if Harvey were buried in Texas, he would have had a well tended grave. W. W.'s grave, wife and two children are on the Johnson Ranch north of Gordon, Texas. I have a feeling Harvey was shipped back to Ionia for burial.

Can you put me in touch with someone who might help solve this mystery which has long been a puzzle around here?

Sincerely,
Leo S. Bielinski

Enc: Book **BACK ROAD TO THURBER** which describes the Johnsons' Texas ventures.

An unsigned, undated letter was received from the Library:

HALL-FOWLER MEMORIAL LIBRARY
IONIA, MICHIGAN 48846

Dear Library User:

The Hall-Fowler Memorial Library houses the following local history collection: Ionia County Cemetery Records, Ionia City and County Directories, Ionia County Histories and Plat Books; Ionia City Newspapers and County Census.

We are sorry that staff time does not permit us to do genealogical research for patrons. However, the Grand Rapids Public Library, in Grand Rapids, Michigan, does maintain a list of professional genealogists who do this research for a fee.

Sincerely Yours,
The staff of the Hall-Fowler Memorial Library

After such negativity from Ionia, Michigan sources, the thought surfaced: *Could the people of Ionia still harbor a grudge for the Johnson family after a hundred years?*

The brothers, W.W. and Harvey Johnson, heavily in debt to Ionia creditors, fled to Texas in 1879. Although W.W. became wealthy in Texas he haughtily refused to pay off some of these old debts, and settled others for as little as 10 cents on the dollar. The Johnson brothers knew what they were doing when they skipped to Texas, for under Texas Law, after ten years' residence in Texas, the Johnsons could not be prosecuted for prior debts. Could the Johnson family's reputation for refusal to pay legal debts have been passed on through three generations, and perhaps been embellished by rumors of the brothers attaining great wealth in Texas? For fear of prosecution in the state of Michigan, the brothers never again set foot in their home town of Ionia, Michigan.

Goaded with these thoughts of a possible long-standing grudge, two angry letters were written to Ionia officials:

24 August 1994

Hall-Fowler Memorial Library
126 E. Main
Ionia, Michigan 48846

    I enclose a check for $1.48 postage. Would you please return the book "THE BACK ROAD TO THURBER" which I previously donated to your library?

I don't understand discourteous ingrates who ignore requests for help.

Leo S. Bielinski, Ph.D.

27 August 1994
To: Ionia Chamber of Commerce
428 West Washington St.
Ionia, Michigan 48846

WHAT IS WRONG WITH YOU PEOPLE IN IONIA?

I received the unsigned, cold form letter from your library which ignored my concerns. Secondly, I donated a valuable book to your library (THE BACK ROAD TO THURBER), thinking the good people of Ionia might enjoy the fascinating story of two former Ionians. But I never even got the courtesy of an acknowledgment of book receipt.

I previously wrote to the Ionia Chamber of Commerce (1989) and to two funeral homes in Ionia. But zero help!

I'll pay somebody $20 if they'll spend fifteen minutes to check Ionia County Cemetery Records at the Library and tell me if Harvey E. Johnson is buried in Ionia. That's all I want; I'm not asking for genealogy! I probably know more about the Johnsons than all the people combined in Ionia.

I don't understand this discourtesy. Is this symptomatic of the times, or is there another deep-lying problem?

Leo S. Bielinski, Ph.D.

Unsigned Reply:

HALL-FOWLER MEMORIAL LIBRARY
IONIA, MICHIGAN 48846

31 August 1994

Dear Mr. L. Bielinski:

Attached is a check for $15.00 for the purchase of "Back Road to Thurber." (This is the average price for books purchased by the library.) It is not the policy of the library to return donations.

I apologize if you are offended by our reply to genealogy requests by mail. We are a small-staffed library and are unable to keep up with such requests.

I checked the Cemetery Indexes and enclose the only listing of a "Harvey Johnson." Again, I apologize for causing you any offense.

Sincerely,
Librarian

The brothers Harvey E. and William W. Johnson began the first coal mine in Thurber, Texas, Erath County in 1886. They had come to Texas in 1879 from Ionia, Michigan to escape creditors and to make a new start. Their General Store and Post Yard on the main line of the Texas & Pacific Rail Road at Strawn, Texas soon thrived as ranchers needed posts and barbed wire to fence in ranges as the railroads expanded westward.[1]

William was nine years older than Harvey, but the two brothers had a unique relationship of trust and confidence between them.[2] Harvey had a common touch with folks and was business-minded, while William was more aloof and an "enterprising man."[3]

Just on the verge of success in their coaling enterprise, Harvey E. died on January 30, 1888 and left everything to William, which again illustrated the deep bond of affection between the brothers.[4]

William wanted to ship Harvey back home to Ionia, Michigan for burial, but because of legal and financial problems, he was advised against this by their Ionia attorney, Albert Williams.[5] Writer Robert Spoede, in his excellent thesis on W. W. Johnson, surmised Harvey was buried near Strawn.[6] With their close relationship, certainly William would have ensured a well-kept grave plot and a fitting monument, two prerequisites which would have been noticeable in any cemeteries near Strawn. And Harvey E. Johnson is not listed in any Cemetery Indexes in Palo Pinto, Eastland or Parker Counties.[7]

On 3 February 1888, four days after Harvey's death, W.W. Johnson had a $226.65 bill for the funeral.[8] and this modest cost would indicate Harvey was not shipped a great distance for burial, perhaps Fort Worth or Dallas at the farthest.

There is no listing for a Harvey E. Johnson in Ionia County, Michigan Cemetery Indexes.[9] Spoede believed the father, Ethan S. might have died in Texas in 1883.[10] Could the father have been visiting the two sons in Texas at the time of his death? If so, then Ethan S. (the father) and Harvey E. might be buried in adjoining graves, but where? The mother, Jane B. Johnson, died in Los Angeles, California in December 1902. There were three girls and four boys in the Johnson family. All sisters married, two remaining in Michigan and one moving to California. The second and fourth brothers were in mental institutes their entire adult lives.[11]

W.W. Johnson and his wife, Anna, had wealth and success in many business ventures, but they carried inordinate grief throughout their lives. Sadly, Anna and her daughter, Fannie, by her first marriage, remained estranged throughout life; Fannie living with an aunt in Denver, Colorado.[12] The Johnson's daughter and son died at early ages. They could not bear having the children buried underground, and they kept the bodies in a mausoleum at the side of the house. William died in 1914 and when Anna died in 1922, an eighteen-foot-square mausoleum of native sandstone was built on the Johnson Ranch, five miles north of Gordon, Texas. The mother's casket was placed on one side, the father's on the other side, the two children in the center, and the crypt was sealed forever.[13]

William W. Johnson's correspondence, some 7,000 pieces,[14] is located at the Southwest Collection at Texas Tech University.

After 100 years, the mystery of Harvey's grave location was finally solved. In 1995 John Wilson of Lone Camp, TX found an old newspaper, the "Gordon Weekly Courier" (May 29, 1903), which stated that Harvey E. Johnson was buried in his hometown of Ionia, Michigan.[15] However, Cemetery Indexes for Ionia do not list Harvey E. Johnson.[16] Could burial in an Ionia Cemetery have been denied the Johnsons because some Ionians in 1903 might have nurtured bad feelings over the Johnsons fleeing to Texas to escape Ionian creditors? Perhaps, the Johnsons might have had to bury in a cemetery outside Ionia. The Gordon newspaper referred to the "Ionia Michigan Standard" of May 21, 1903 which reported that "Mrs. Ethan S. (Jane Whipple) Johnson died in Los Angeles, California on Dec. 8, 1902 at the home of her daughter, Mrs. E.G. Faulkner. Her son, William Whipple Johnson, was present at her death. Mrs. Johnson's body was embalmed and placed in the family mausoleum (in Strawn) with that of her son Harvey (who died in Texas many years ago) until Mrs. Dean (another daughter) who was in poor health was well enough to return to Ionia. Mrs. Dean returned to

Ionia on April 23rd with the remains of her mother and brother Harvey for burial beside Mrs. Dean's father Ethan S. Johnson."

This account also noted that Mrs. Jane Whipple Johnson was the granddaughter of William Whipple, one of the signers of the Declaration of Independence.

While a "Family Mausoleum" in Strawn, Texas was indicated as Harvey Johnson's repository, no mention was made that W. W. Johnson's two children were also in this mausoleum at this time. This newspaper account was the first indication that Harvey Johnson's remains were in a mausoleum in Strawn for 15 years, from 1888 to 1903. But this family mausoleum also contained the bodies of daughter Marion (1885) and son Harvey (1894. All previous written accounts referred to a small mausoleum for the children, but Harvey was never mentioned in connection with the children's mausoleum. For example, "After an undertaker had prepared the child (Marion) for burial they kept her in an upstairs bedroom where Mrs. Johnson dressed the body in one lacy thing after another. In the meantime, outside the window, a small brick house was erected and when completed Marion's body was placed in a casket and put into this miniature mausoleum."

When the second child, William Harvey, died in 1894 "...Bill was dressed in his fairy costume and placed in the doll house by his little sister."[17] Either the children's mausoleum was large enough to contain the bodies of the two children and two adults, Harvey and Mrs. Johnson, or perhaps Harvey's mausoleum was a room in the Johnson's large home. Upon daughter Marion's death, W. W. Johnson cried, "God Almighty can take the lives of my children, but He cannot have their bodies."[18] And the earth's soil never touched the coffin of Johnson, or any of his immediate family, for their final interment was in a mausoleum on the Johnson Ranch north of Gordon, Texas.

However, in November 1995, one hundred and seven years after death, Harvey E. Johnson's grave site location was not specifically known by Thurber historians, except to say that it was in some cemetery in or near Ionia, Michigan.

HARVEY JOHNSON'S GRAVE,
HIGHLAND PARK CEMETERY, IONIA, MI.

Finally, since Ionia, Michigan officials had not been helpful Barbara Arends and Karen Coulson of Glenn and Saranac, Michigan, respectively, went to the Ionia, Michigan Library for research. In Cemetery Records they did not find a listing for Harvey E. Johnson, but there was a listing for Stephen Johnson. From an 1870 census, they correctly assumed that Stephen and Harvey Johnson were brothers. Therefore, since Stephen was buried in Highland Park Cemetery (Sect. 4, lot 127), Harvey most likely would be buried nearby. But alas! The Library Staff, "Three pickle-pussed people who didn't seem to like us, wouldn't let us use the library phone to call the Highland Park Cemetery caretaker. We had to find a pay phone up the street."

Thus, the search for Harvey E. Johnson's grave was concluded. Harvey E. Johnson's grave was found in the Johnson-Dean-Miller plot in Ionia, Michigan. The long, difficult, frustrating search for Harvey's grave was finally over.

THE SEARCH FOR HARVEY JOHNSON'S GRAVE NOTES

1. Robert W. Spoede, "William Whipple Johnson: an Enterprising Man," Abilene: MA Thesis, Hardin-Simmons University, 1968, pp. 21, 33, 34.

2. Leo S. Bielinski, The Back Road to Thurber, Baird, TX: Joy Presswork Collection, 1993, p. 63.

3. Spoede, p. 57.

4. Ibid, p. 56.

5. Ibid, p. 56.

6. Ibid, p. 57.

7. Cemetery Tombstone Inscriptions, Palo Pinto and Parker Counties, Weatherford Public Library, Weatherford, TX.

8. Spoede, p. 56.

9. Cemetery Index for Ionia County, Michigan, Hall-Fowler Memorial Library, Ionia, Michigan.

10. Spoede, p. 8.

11. Ibid, p. 9.

12. Bielinski, p. 157.

13. Ibid, p. 159.

14. Spoede, p. vii.

15. The Gordon Courier, May 29, 1903. John Wilson, Lone Camp, Texas.

16. Cemetery Index, Ionia County, Michigan.

17. Mary Whatley Clark, The Palo Pinto Story, Fort Worth, Manney Co., 1956, p. 153.

18. Clark, p. 153.

THURBER 1921 – A LOCKOUT OR A STRIKE?

By 1920 most railroads had changed to oil, and with the discovery of the nearby Ringer Oil Field, the Texas Pacific Coal and Oil Company's primary focus was now on oil. After thirty-some years, the Company was ready to phase out its Thurber coaling operation

In 1921 the company proposed a $2.50 per day pay cut, a 33% reduction. The union countered with $1.50. On May 1, 1921 the company closed the mines.[1] Since its contract with the union still had a year, there is general agreement among writers that the Company reneged on its contract with the union.[2] But there is misunderstanding about subsequent events: that the miners went on "strike,"[3] that all the mines permanently closed at this time because of the "strike"[4] and that all miners were immediately evicted from Thurber.[5]

But the Company still had coal contracts to fulfill at this time. No problem. Only three mines were in operation in 1921: #10, New #1 and New #3.[6] Close down New # 1, hire "scab" labor,[7] evict those not willing to work at reduced wages[8] and work # 10 and New #3 to satisfy existing coal contracts.[9]

This pay cut was devastating for most miners with families because they could not live on this. They were forced out of company homes (Fig. 1) and moved into "Tent City," an encampment of WWI tents set up by the union a half-mile north of Thurber (Figs. 2 and 3).

151

IMPORTANT NOTICE

ALL PARTIES OCCUPYING COMPANY HOUSES AND WHO HAVE NOT PAID THEIR RENT, WATER, LIGHT AND GAS CHARGES, ARE HEREBY GIVEN FURTHER NOTICE TO CALL AT THE OFFICE AND MAKE SETTLEMENT OF THESE ACCOUNTS, AND FAILING TO DO SO ON OR BEFORE SATURDAY SEPTEMBER 24, 1921, WATER, LIGHTS AND GAS WILL BE DISCONTINUED WITHOUT FURTHER NOTICE, AFTER OCTOBER 1, 1921.

Texas Pacific Coal and Oil Co.
September 10, 1921

FIG. 1 – TEXAS PACIFIC COAL AND OIL CO. NOTICE.
THIS STATEMENT IN EFFECT, WAS AN EVICTION
NOTICE FOR SOME THURBER RESIDENTS

FIG. 2 – TENT CITY, JUST NORTH OF THURBER, OCT. 1921

FIG. 3 – SOME OF THE CHILDREN LIVING IN TENT CITY

Gladys Bridier Bradford remembers living in Tent City:

"I was eleven when we had to move to Tent City. There were a good many people there. Sanitary conditions weren't too good. Everybody got water out of water barrels. I got real sick, almost died with typhoid. It was in the spring. Then our tent blew down on top of us, and Dewey Mann let us move into his house over there by John Dow's. I finally got over the typhoid fever there. A doctor from Thurber was treating me, but Mama asked him to send another doctor. So Dr. Binney came and said I was doing fine; to feed me. But Mama was afraid that feeding me would make me worse. But she did and I got well. And then we moved to the mine fields in Illinois. After several months, we moved to the coal mines at Hartshorne, Oklahoma. And finally back to Thurber. Daddy wrote a letter to Mace Oyler in Thurber, and Mace wrote Daddy that he had a job for him."

When the Company closed the mines in 1921, the miners thought the company would come to its senses in a few months and rehire the miners.[11] But it was not to be, and many miners went back to the "Old Country." The union found employment for some in the coal fields of Illinois[12] and others moved to California and other states.

Fortunately, at this time the Volstead Act (prohibiting alcoholic beverages) was in force, and about 200 ex-miners who lived in Thurber Junction turned to "bootlegging" for subsistence.[13] With the nearby Ranger Oil Field, this endeavor, although illegal, was the salvation for many ex-miners. Although all nationalities were involved in making illegal beverages, most were Italians. And they were noted for their "grappo" (grape-raisin) whisky. There was none of the big city gangsterism associated with this activity; "Just a way of makin' a livin'."

The UMW was spending $65,000. a month to sustain Tent City.[14] In April 1922 the UMW called a nationwide strike and funds to Tent City were shut off. But Lawrence Santi, an official of the Italian local, continued signing his name on vouchers for aid to UMW members.[15] After a few more months Tent City was abandoned.

Even to this day, there is the misconception that Thurber miners went on strike in 1921.[16] But Lawrence Santi harshly criticized any one who suggested this, and adamantly swore it was a lockout.[17] Santi's views are strongly reinforced by John Bagatti of Highwood, Illinois who was a miner in Thurber in 1921:

> **"...There was Lorenzo Santi from Pieve (Italy). He was a good man... He's the one that made the contract to the company and to the working man... In 1918, Santi became president of the UMW local in Thurber, Texas, and later served as mayor of Mingus, where he settled after being run out of Thurber during a lockout by the Texas and Pacific Coal and Oil Company in 1921... They called this a strike in 1921, March 30. It was not a strike! Positively!... That was a lockout... And there is no question about it because we had a**

contract with a coal company to run a year beyond that date...
But the year prior to the expiration of the contract, the
company sought to force a reduction... That's an absolute fact.
In other words, they forced, not a strike, but a lockout. They
are the ones who turned to striking. They were trying to tell the
people that the miners struck which was an absolute
falsehood... You see they attempted, they endeavored to
operate those mines with strike breakers... Incidentally, I was
the second man to be shoved out of there. See, we lived in a
company property, and I got notice to get out of there. They
didn't use very much diplomacy..."[18]

*lockout – the refusal by an employer to allow his employees to
come into work unless they agree to his terms.[19]*

If one were willing to work at lower wages for the company, he
could remain in Company housing. And there were enough miners to
work #10 and New #3 until 1926. "Scab" was a dirty word and there
were many arguments and fist fights between "scabs" and union
men, and even school kids fought when one called the other's Dad a
"scab."[20]

Because of individual and family needs, some miners were
forced to accept the company's pay cut. Although the union shipped
200 Mexican miners back to Mexico.[21] It has been known that the
bulk of the "scab" labor force was Mexican.[22] And this view is
supported by Church Baptismal statistics. In the five years preceding
1921, there were a total 404 Baptisms; 168 Mexicans (41%) and 236
all other nationalities (59%). In the five years following 1921, there
were a total 217 Baptisms; 155 Mexicans (71%) and only 62 all other
nationalities (29%). Thus, after 1921 the number of Mexican
Baptisms decreased only slightly (168-155), but the number of
Baptisms for all other nationalities dropped 74% (236-62).[23]

In 1922, a year after the distressing 1921 events at Thurber, about 50 workers at the nearby Thurber Junction car repair yards, two miles north of Thurber, became part of a nationwide railway strike. With Thurber still boiling and its effects rippling throughout the area, this railroad strike at Thurber Junction had violence and a killing.[24] The T & P Railroad harshly reacted by permanently closing this repair facility. With the closing of coal mines, the RR repair yards, the brick plant in 1931, the repeal of the Volstead Act in 1933 and with the Great Depression in full force, Thurber was one of the hardest-hit areas in the country. It is hard to imagine by today's standards, that a family in the 1930's subsisted on WPA (Work's Progress Administration) wages of a dollar a day ($24 a month) for pick and shovel work. Skilled labor, like carpenters, brick masons, truck drivers and time keepers made $36. a month. These were times that broke the spirit of man but the work got the men outdoors, working together and sharing their problems. The boys helped by hunting and fishing and trapping for pelts.

Some men went to work tearing down Thurber's brickyard, and were paid $1.50 per thousand for cleaning bricks. When the bricks were soft-mortared, a man might make $1.50 a day. Charley Hamilton of Thurber Junction (Mingus) supervised the razing of the brickyard.

But hard times did not end for this area until WWII.

THURBER 1921 – A LOCKOUT OR A STRIKE NOTES

1. John S. Spratt, <u>Thurber Texas</u>, Austin: University of Texas Press, 1986, p. 116.

2. Ibid. Also Hardman, p. 58 and Gentry, p. 99.

3. Weldon Hardman, <u>Fire in a Hole!</u>, Gordon, TX: Thurber Historical Association, 1991, p. 58. Also Gentry, p. 122.

4. State Historical Marker on brick smokestack at Thurber, 1969. Also Gentry, p. 97 and Spratt, p. 116.

5. Spratt, p. 116.

6. S. M. Greenidge, "Report on Coal Reserves of Texas Pacific Coal and Oil Co.", Fort Worth, 1953, p. 16.

7. Mary Jane Gentry, "Thurber: the Life and Death of a Texas Town," Austin: Master's Thesis, University of Texas, 1946, p. 122.

8. Spratt, p. 116.

9. Greenidge, p. 16.

10. Gladys Bridier Bradford to Leo S. Bielinski, Strawn, TX: Interview 19 Dec 1994.

11. Hardman, p. 59.

12. Ibid.

13. Leo S. Bielinski, "Beer, Booze, Bootlegging and Bocci Ball", Abilene: West Texas Historical Association Year Book, Vol. LVIX, 1983, p. 78.

14. Spratt, p. 117.

15. George Green, Transcribed Interview with Mr. Lawrence Santi", Arlington: Univ. of Texas at Arlington, TX Labor Archives, Feb. 1974, p. 21.

16. Hardman, p. 58. Also Gentry, p. 122.

17. Green, p. 16.

18. Adria Bernardi, "Houses with Names, the Italian Immigrants of Highwood, Illinois", Urbana: University of Illinois Press, p. 105.

19. Webster's New World Dictionary, 1966, p. 861.

20. Tony Sadver to Leo S. Bielinski, Strawn, TX: Interview June 1991.

21. Spratt, p. 118.

22. Gino Solognani to Leo S. Bielinski, Mingus, TX: Interview Aug 1989.

23. St. Barbara's Baptismal Records located at St. Rita's, Ranger TX.

24. Spratt, p. 122.

INTERESTING THURBER SITES
(STATE HISTORICAL MARKERS IN THURBER)

THURBER'S SNAKE SALOON

Thurber's Snake Saloon was the largest and busiest saloon between Fort Worth and El Paso,[1] and saloons were always a part of Thurber's panorama because the Eastern European miners were traditionally accustomed to beverages. But R.D. Hunter, President of Texas and Pacific Coal Co., had several problems with saloons in and around Thurber. First, there was a legal fight between Hunter and the lessee of the Snake Saloon, Lawson,[2] then a gang fight in the Drug Store between Hunter, Lawson et al,[3] next arguments with Jimmy Grant over Grant's saloon east of Thurber,[4] a court battle when Hunter closed the road in front of Bruce and Stewart's Saloon,[5] irate miners when Hunter cut wages to $1/ton because miners were patronizing Bruce and Stewart's Saloon,[6] union activities at Bruce and Stewart's saloon etc.[7]

The first Snake Saloon was a two-story brick building between the Drug Store and the Livery Stable; the saloon on the bottom floor and a lodge hall on the top floor.[8] The Snake had a mahogany horseshoe bar which could handle a hundred men at a time. This was a man's domain, off limits to women; no dance floor, no dancing girls and no gambling.[9] The Company also built a saloon on Italian Hill, "The Lizard," to accommodate the Italian and Polish miners.[10]

When Erath County went "dry" in 1904, the Company built a 40 by 120-foot new Snake Saloon just inside of "wet" Palo Pinto County, a quarter mile north of downtown Thurber.[11] This Snake Saloon had a very long straight bar. There were no seats; the Company knew more men could be served standing than lounging at tables.[12] Sheds and arbors with benches were built outside the saloon

158

where different groups and nationalities gathered and drank.[13] There were songs of the "Old Country," bragging and fistfights. Bruce and Stewart's Saloon, where Union talk took place, was a few hundred yards north of the new Snake Saloon.

The "Beer Business" was big business for the Company. On week days four bartenders were required, and on weekends and holidays it took eight or ten men to serve the thirsty miners.[14] There was plenty y of whisky and wine, but beer was the preferred beverage and could be purchased by the glass, pitcher, bucket or keg.[15]

A large cold storage warehouse was adjacent to the saloon but next to the railroad track, and beer and wine was unloaded from railroad cars to the warehouse.[16] On busy days an almost constant rumble could be heard from beer and wine kegs rolling down the ramp from the warehouse to the saloon. The saloon's average daily take was more than $1,000, and in 1914 the Company bought 11,935 barrels of beer from Fort Worth Brewing Co., equivalent to 160 carloads.[17] This brewery used "nut" coal from Thurber's mines in its brewing operations, coal for which the miners received no pay. The Company would trade a carload of "nut" coal for a carload of beer. Before the Coal Miners' Strike of 1903, it was strangely incongruous that the miners got nothing for the "nut" coal they mined, but they had to pay for the beer which the "nut" coal helped brew.[18]

The Snake Saloon closed when the Palo Pinto County voted "dry" in 1916, but this was not the end of alcoholic beverages for the Thurber area. When some of the coal mines closed in 1921 the unemployed miners who owned homes in nearby Thurber Junction turned to bootlegging. Their specialty was "grappo" whisky which was made from raisins, and Thurber Junction (Mingus) was nicknamed "Grappo Junction."[19] With the nearby Ranger Oil Boom on, bootlegging was prosperous for the Thurber locale.

With the repeal of the Volstead Act in 1933, several saloons immediately opened in Grant's Town and Thurber Junction. But the Snake Saloon was never reopened because at this time Thurber was being torn down. The final destiny of Thurber's famous Horse Shoe bar remains unknown.

THURBER CEMETERY

This 9.1 acre cemetery is diagonally bisected by the Palo Pinto/Erath County line such that the cemetery is in two counties. The oldest grave in this 100 year-old cemetery is that of an African-American girl, Eva Chapman, born and died __ 21, 1890.[1]

Over 1,000 people are buried herein, but more than 700 are in unmarked graves, indicated by white plastic crosses. Their names are listed on the large monument near the entrance.[2] Why so many unmarked graves? As long as Thurber was active families knew grave locations and lovingly tended them. When Thurber was abandoned in the 1930's the intent was to return with permanent markers. But it never worked out that way.

The cemetery has three distinct sections: the African-American, the Catholic and the White Protestant; each with its own entrance. The east gate, in use today, was for the African-Americans, the north gate for the Catholics and the south gate for the White Protestants.[3]

In the African-American Section there are two identical, adjacent tombstones for Mary Green, wives of Jack Green. But ages are different. Jack was careful to not show partiality to either wife.[4]

An eight-foot weatherworn wooden cross in the Catholic Section marks the grave of Anthony Bascilli. This man dug his own grave, lined it with bricks and marked it with the cross. To ensure that those shoveling dirt in his grave would be careful, he said he had hidden pints of whisky in the dirt he dug out. A new suit and new shoes were placed in the foot of his casket. A metal door was hinged over the casket, a few feet of dirt was shoveled in, and then another metal door with lock was placed over this and covered with remaining dirt. A key was dropped down a pipe to the casket.[5] One can only imagine Bascilli's conception of Resurrection Day: he certainly wanted to be presentable and the first one out!

Over half the graves are children less than two years old.[6] Babies were sometimes buried in shoe boxes.[7] There were several instances when one family buried three children in one year. The Castaldo burial plot in the Catholic Section (low metal fence and tall four-sided marker) has graves for three children who all died within a few days of each other.[8] There were diseases which are not common today: diphtheria, scarlet fever, whooping cough and malaria.

A dozen years ago, cemetery gates were opened to permit cattle to graze in the cemetery, and to this day damage is still being corrected. One of the tombstones knocked over by cattle was that of Rev. J.B. Dodson, 1865-1919. Research by local Methodist ministers discovered an old-time circuit riding preacher who had briefly served as pastor of Thurber Methodist Church. Although born in Missouri and dying in Dallas, this minister wanted to be buried in Thurber. In the Fall of 1993, the Methodist Church honored Rev. Dodson by placing a Circuit Rider emblem on his tombstone (preacher with Bible on horseback).[9]

Mike McCounnla. Sandstone marker. Mike was proud of his union membership in Brick, Tile and Terra Cotta Workers (B T T). In upper left corner is union symbol, but "B" is backward.

Georgie Milligan. Concrete marker. "As yo(sic) are now, so once was I, As I am now so yo(sic) must be. So trust in God and follow me."

A beautifully detailed weathered sandstone marks the graves of two Croatian sisters, Marija and Olga Kalcicrodje. There are three other similar sandstone markers in the cemetery, all undoubtedly carved by the same meticulous craftsman. The words are in Croatian: "Here are resting in peace two sisters, Olga and Marija (dates). This marker erected by their parents. 'Let the soil be light for them.' "[10]

Because of rocks in the cemetery, particularly in the African-American Section, graves were hard to dig, and sometimes dynamite was used to blast out graves. When one heard a dynamite blast emanating from the direction of the cemetery, the question might be asked, "I wonder who died?"[11]

GORDON RESIDENCE IN THURBER

This house was built by the T. & P. Coal Co. in 1912 for it's General Manager, W. K. Gordon, and his family: wife Fay Kearby, son W. K. Gordon, Jr. and daughter Louise. Mr. Gordon resided here during Thurber's years of successful production in the coal and brick industries,[1] as well as his discovery of the Ranger Oil Field in 1917,[2] for which he was recognized nationally. At the time, Ranger was the biggest oil boom in the history of the world. Production in 1919 was $90,000,000 worth of oil and in 1920 $100,000,000.[3]

The house was uniquely designed; one of a kind for Thurber, being a two-story "extended Craftsman bungalow...with an extensive porch area."[4] The lower floor consisted of a living room, dining room, breakfast room, two bedrooms, two bathrooms, kitchen and screened porch. The second floor consisted of three bedrooms and two baths.

Equally distinctive was the well kept horseshoe-shaped yard, surrounded by a three-foot high picket fence, which many children found to be a playground. Roller skating on the seventy yard long concrete sidewalk was popular. There were croquet and two grass tennis courts in the back and east yard which substituted for a boxing arena and a football field as well[5].

Under-house cellars are not common in the south, but the Gordon House had a cellar. Another unique feature was central heating with steam radiators.

After the T. & P. Oil Co. moved its offices to Fort Worth in 1933 and most of Thurber was demolished, the Gordon house was called the "Guest House." It was used as a recreational lodge for company executives who hunted and fished in Thurber.[6]

THURBER'S OPERA HOUSE

Thurber's Opera House was the center of entertainment in the community with touring operatic and dramatic troupes, dress balls, magicians, badger fights, school functions, silent movies, local talent and meetings.[1]

The Opera House was dedicated in October 1896 with a brilliant ball "...beautiful ladies, handsomely attired, and gallant men ... getting from their few hours all of life." A grand march, waltzes, two-steps, schottisches, polkas and minuet dances. "...and it was 3 a.m. when the orchestra struck up the 'Home Sweet Home' waltz."[2]

The Opera House overflowed with miners and other workers when T and P Coal Co. President Edgar Marston and union officials announced settlement of the 1903 miners' strike which marked the beginning of the labor movement in the Southwest.[3] Marston and union officials arrived in Marston's private railroad car on the rail spur which ran through downtown Thurber to only 50 yards from the Opera House.[4] And when "big-time" shows came to Thurber, actors and singers lived in Pullman coaches on this railroad siding.[5] Some of Thurber's famous "badger" versus bulldog fights were staged in the Opera House, and distinguished guests were accorded the "honor" of releasing the "fierce badger."[6] The "badger" turned out to be a chamber pot.

The Opera House had a seating capacity of 655. There was a spacious lobby, private boxes, a dress circle, parquet circle and a balcony. The 30 x 50-foot stage was bordered by several background drops from a 28-foot loft, three dressing rooms and an orchestra pit.[7] The building was heated by steam and lighted by 136 electric lights with a center light cluster.[8]

After the Hotel Knox burned in 1907, this section (parquet) of the Opera House replaced the ballroom of the Hotel Knox as the scene of social activities for company executives and their friends.[9] Seats (actually chairs) in the balcony and boxes were not attached to the floor.[10] "The furniture in this building ... was made in Thurber, and speaks well for the capacity of the appliances there and the ability of the workmen."[11]

Joe Kostiha, a native of Czechoslovakia who came to Thurber to work in the mines, said, "You could hear opera companies just like in New York City, here in the old days. Metropolitan Opera companies traveling between Fort Worth-Dallas to El Paso on the T and P RR made regular stops for performances here."[12]

When motion pictures became popular, the Opera House was converted to a movie theater.[13] A player piano was installed in the orchestra pit to accompany the silent movies.[14] With the advent of sound films, the movie theater was relocated in the Presbyterian Church building.[15]

On 4 September 1930, the roof of the Opera House was damaged by fire which swept Marston Hall, the Fire Hall and the Baldridge home.[16] Shortly thereafter, the venerable old Opera House was scrapped for lumber.

THURBER'S HOTEL KNOX AND MINING OFFICE

Thurber's Hotel Knox was advertised as "The best Hotel west of Fort Worth."[1] It was built about 1895 by the Texas and Pacific Coal Co. at the northwest corner of the square. "At Hotel Knox ... many of the mine office and mercantile department clerks make their home in a charmingly located, well constituted hotel where everything is kept neat as a pin, and the service is unexceptional."[2] But the hotel also accommodated travelers with business in Thurber.[3] And most of the social events took place here: dinners, grand balls, and other social gatherings. It was to the Hotel Knox that Thurber General Manager W.K. Gordon brought his bride after their marriage.[4]

The Hotel had electricity throughout, hot, cold and mineral water hot baths at all hours, flowing mineral water in the yard and special rates to opera troupes.[5]

Since Thurber was three miles south of the main rail line, a Concord Stage from the Hotel Knox met all passenger trains at Thurber Junction (Mingus).[6] This was the last regularly scheduled stage coach run in America.[7] This stage was described as "A modern looking stage, drawn by four sleek horses and driven by a polite Jehu (a fast coachman), smartly dressed, conveys the traveler at a brisk pace to the town ... The impression you get is that things are done in order and up-to-date fashion at Thurber's Hotel Knox with the comforts of a first class city inn."[8]

When the Hotel Knox burned in 1907, a new hotel (Plummer Hotel) was built to the north of the Mining Office, the Mining Office being between the two hotels. The new Hotel was said to be superior in construction and elegance to the Hotel Knox, but with the demise of the Hotel Knox, it seemed a way of life had gone that could not be replaced.[9]

To accommodate travelers who could not get rooms at the Knox, or who could not meet train schedules, the company also owned the Junction Hotel and Restaurant in Thurber Junction, two miles north, near the Train Depot.[10]

The Mining Office was located between the Knox and Plummer Hotels.[11] General Manager W.K. Gordon's office was on the bottom floor of this two-story brick building, as were the offices of the Paymaster and the Maintenance Supervisor. The Company's Legal Staff was housed on the second floor.[12] Most of Thurber's activities were directed from supervisory personnel in this building.

ST. BARBARA'S CHURCH AT THURBER

With the recruitment of Eastern European miners, Catholic Mass in Thurber became a necessity, for through the Mass the immigrants felt a communion with home and loved ones thousands of miles away.[1] Periodic masses were held from about 1890 to 1892 in some company buildings. Mission priests were Fathers Litwora from Bremond, Texas; Brickley from Abilene, Texas; and Fabrio from the Dallas Diocese.[2] The Texas and Pacific Coal Co. built and owned all buildings in Thurber, including churches. The church was completed in late 1892[3] and the company called it St. Thuribus, probably because "Thuribus" sounded similar to "Thurber."[4] But within a few years, the name was appropriately changed to St. Barbara's; the patroness saint of miners.

How did a lady saint become patroness saint of miners? St. Barbara was a 2nd century martyr. At the age of twelve she told her father she intended to follow the Christian religion. The father was horrified because he was a Roman official and a pagan, so he locked her in a tower to make her change her mind. One year, two years, three years; Barbara's faith grew even stronger. In desperation, he went before the Roman officials to confess: "My daughter is a Christian, what shall I do?" The answer was, "Kill her!" On the way to kill his daughter, the father was struck and killed by lightning, followed by a big blast of thunder. Thus, the blast of thunder was associated with the blast from explosives used in mining and quarrying, and St. Barbara became the patroness saint of miners, quarry workers, artillerymen, rock masons and brick layers.[5]

The first Baptism was Antonin Wierzowiecki, 22 January 1893.[6] Father A.M. Dynia performed 39 Baptisms from 21 Sept 1894 to Feb 1895 and was probably the first assigned pastor. Fathers Kwoka and J.B. Etschenberg served from 1895 to 1896. Father Dolje, a Dutch-American priest (Dec 1896-Oct 1903), was the fourth assigned priest.[7] The company felt Father Dolje was too actively involved in the miners' strike of 1903, and they asked that he be replaced. The Bishop had little choice because the company owned the church building.[8] Father Dolje and the next pastor, Father H.J. Baker (Oct 1903-Feb 1909), were greatly assisted by Father Merendino. The 1910 Census showed eighteen different nationalities in Thurber. Other priests whose names appear on Baptismal records were Fathers Fabrio, Ardus, Kowalski, Gagliardoni and Kew.

Father DeLuca was a colorful, outspoken priest who was pastor from Feb 1909 to Nov 1918. He had little patience with late-to-Mass parishioners, always arriving about sermon time. One Sunday they marched in late again. Father stopped his sermon, looked pleadingly heavenward up towards God and said, "Oh God, you give me jackasses, and I'll give you jackasses right back."[9] An adjunct to the church, Hunter Academy, was established in 1894 by the Sisters of the Incarnate Word of San Antonio and was named after the founder of Thurber, R.D. Hunter.[10] In addition to regular classes, the sisters held night school for boys who worked in the mines and English classes for the foreign-born.[11] The school was closed in 1923, and at that time there were 168 pupils and six sisters.[12]

Father Niedziela was pastor at Thurber from Nov 1918 to June 1920. Then Father Herkert June 1920-Oct 1923, and Father Kline Oct 1923-Dec 1935.[13] Father Corcoran (1936-1941) supervised the moving of St. Barbara's two miles to the north to Mingus, when Thurber was being dismantled. When moved, the church was sawed in two, each half moved separately, then rejoined in Mingus.[14]

The company-owned Thurber Merchandise and Mercantile Co. offered "Service from Cradle to Grave," and this included coffins and embalming. But virtually all bodies were without embalming because of cost, and burial took place the same day or the next day following death. There was no funeral parlor for visitation, and friends and family sat overnight with the corpse in the home. In many cases if the deceased was a boarder, home visitation was impractical, and the body might be left in the 4 x 10-foot recess on the left side of the church.[15]

There were about 2,500 Baptisms and 335 Funeral Masses in St. Barbara's.[16] During St. Barbara's Thurber days, clocks, watches, radios and TV's were not available for time checks as in modern times. When St. Barbara's bell was first heard on Sunday that meant: "Thirty minutes before Mass, get dressed." The next bell was fifteen minutes before Mass: "Get moving toward church." The last bell, five minutes before Mass, meant "Get in your pew."[17]

In Mingus after 1970, the church was rarely used and was in disrepair. In August 1993, St. Barbara's was moved back home to

Thurber. Today, it has been restored as a nondenominational church with a mandate that only religious activities be conducted in this venerable old church. After two moves, and one hundred years, St. Barbara's Church proudly stands, ready for the next hundred years.

THURBER'S NEW YORK HILL

There were two distinct historical eras in Thurber: the Coal Era (1888-1917) and the Oil Era (1917-1933). New York Hill was associated with the Oil Era and was so named because many residents on this hill had been transferred to Thurber from the company's New York office[1] after W.K. Gordon brought in the nearby Ranger Oil Field in October 1917 ("The Oil Field that Won WWI").[2] Some Thurberites daily commuted fifteen miles to the oil activity at Ranger, and this meant a challenging trip in climbing Ranger Hill, particularly in weather and if the car were a Model T Ford with only two forward gears.[3]

To accommodate these oil operation workers, the Texas and Pacific Coal and Oil Co. spent $250,000 for thirty-one homes on New York Hill,[4] about $8,000 a house. This contrasts sharply with the cost of coal miners' houses built twenty years earlier at a cost of about $200.[5] A half mile long brick sidewalk ran from downtown Thurber, stair-stepped up New York Hill, then continued southward to the homes on the hill. The original brick steps up the Hill are still in place. Edgar L. Marston, President of the Company, wanted to build a forty room hotel on the Hill, but could not find a backer.[6]

The New Yorkers also brought a more sophisticated lifestyle to Thurber: a nine-hole golf course, Club privileges at Thurber's Big Lake, a bowling alley and many parties and dances[7] at the Thurber Club where big bands like Lawrence Welk, Jan Garber and Jack

Amelung played.[8] The Roaring Twenties and Prohibition embraced Thurber's Oil Era.

The street up New York Hill was called Church Street because of three churches on this street: the Baptist and Negro Churches at the base of the Hill and the Episcopal Church on top of the Hill.[9]

By 1933 the Ranger Oil Boom had fizzled out, and Thurber was being dismantled. The fine homes on New York Hill were sold for $250 and moved away,[10] but the name "New York Hill" remained.

THURBER'S COAL MINES

At the base of what would later be called New York Hill, the Johnson brothers, W.W. (1843-1914) and Harvey E. (1852-1888) in the Fall of 1886, sank the first coal shaft to a depth of 65 feet.[1] Their company was the "Johnson Coal Mining Co." and the settlement around the mine was called "Johnsonville."[2] Because of labor and financial problems, W.W. Johnson sold his coaling interests to R.D. Hunter (1833-1902) and the Texas and Pacific Coal Co. in the Fall of 1888, and the community was renamed "Thurber", after one of the investors.[3] By providing a reliable coal supply to the railroads for 30 years, Thurber coal helped open up the Southwest when the railroads began their westward expansion.[4]

There were 2,500 coal miners of 18 nationalities, predominantly Italians, with Poles the second most prevalent group.[5] There were 16 mines which generally ran westward from Thurber.[6] The Miners' Strike of 1903 asserted the preeminence of the United Mine Workers Union; the unions now had "clout" over management, and this was consequential for the labor movement in the Southwest.[7] With this strike, every worker in Thurber belonged to a union, and Thurber became the first totally unionized city in America.[8]

By 1921 most railroads had changed to oil and Thurber's coaling operations were severely curtailed, the last mine closing in 1927.[9]

After his Thurber coal venture, W.W. Johnson, "The Father of the Texas Coal Industry," became involved in several other coal mining operations, mainly in the nearby Lyra-Strawn area.[10]

THURBER BRICK PLANT

Thurber General Manager W.K. Gordon examined the shale mud on his boots and persuaded R.D. Hunter, President of Texas and Pacific Coal Co., to test the brick-making qualities of the shale hills around Thurber.[1]

Hunter's St. Louis friends James Green, owner of LaClede Fire Clay Co., and ceramic engineer L.W. Rumsey visited Thurber in February 1897[2] and in March 1897 the Green and Hunter Brick Company was incorporated with a stock of $100,000. By the end of summer dry-pressed bricks were being produced. The company's original machinery consisted of three Ross-Keller six-mould brick presses powered by a Corliss steam engine. The engine was nicknamed "Old Hunter" after R.D. Hunter.[3]

The first brick kilns were built of unfired bricks held together with shale mortar. Each kiln was about 20 by 60 feet with a row of coal-burning fireboxes running the length of the kiln on both sides. The kilns were filled with bricks so that each would be exposed to direct heat until properly baked.[4] In 1916 the kilns were fired with gas from nearby gas fields.[5]

Prior to the establishment of the Thurber Brick Plant, LaClede bricks were shipped in by rail from St. Louis and used in constructing the brick plant and other structures in Thurber.[6] Thurber bricks paved hundreds of miles of streets and highways throughout

Texas, including portions of the old Bankhead Highway (US 80), Austin's Congress Avenue, and in Fort Worth, Camp Bowie Boulevard, Main Street, North Main and the Stockyards. Thurber bricks were also used in constructing the Galveston Seawall.[7]

The Brick Plant was one-half mile southeast of downtown Thurber and the shale was initially taken from the hill adjacent to the plant, but in 1903 a better grade of shale was found on a hill one mile north of the plant.[8] This hill was "Shale Pit Mountain" on maps, but locally, it was called "Steam Shovel Mountain" because a giant railroad mounted steam shovel loaded the shale onto motor cars.[9]

Thurber's brick operation covered five acres and employed 150 men. Each working day 80,000 paving bricks were produced.[10]

"They moved a mountain at Thurber,
Steam shovels turned the trick,
They burned the kilns, turned the hills,
Into millions of vitrified bricks."[11]

After the Strike of 1903, the Brick Workers' Union gained the right to put the union logo on each brick: an imbedded triangle with a "B", "T" and a "T" at each apex, Brick, Tile, and Terra cotta workers.[12]

By 1930 the Great Depression had curtailed road building, asphalt was recognized as a superior paving material and the Thurber plant was closed in 1931.[13] A Breckenridge, TX salvage company, bossed by Charlie Hamilton, tore the plant down brick by brick, the machinery and scrap metal ending up in Japan.[14] In 1936, at the height of the Great Depression, workers were paid $1.50 a thousand to clean the mortar off the bricks.[15] The Brick Plant's smokestack was demolished March 29, 1937. Forty sticks of dynamite were placed under the base by Charlie Hamilton. The stack which required

60 days in construction, tumbled in six seconds.[16] And Thurber's brick operation, which had made forty different kinds of bricks, came to an end.[17]

THURBER'S BIG LAKE AND DAIRY

From 1886 to 1891 the water situation in Thurber was acute, and water was hauled in from ponds by wagons, and by railroad tank cars.[1] To ensure a good water supply for a growing city, a 20 acre lake, the "Little Lake," was built in 1891 a few hundred yards south of the town square.[2] But by 1896 Thurber outgrew the Little Lake, and General Manager W.K. Gordon designed and built the "Big Lake", a mile southeast of Thurber.[3] This 150 acre lake provided good water for the life of Thurber. All houses had running water and washhouses with showers were provided at the mines.[4]

The lake was stocked with a variety of fish, and Texas and Pacific Coal Co. President, R.D. Hunter, organized "R.D. Hunter Fishing and Boating Club" for company executives and staff.[5] Boating and fishing were also allowed on the Little Lake, which was open to anyone, but to hunt or fish on the Big Lake, one had to be a member of the club.[6] Swimming was prohibited at the Big Lake, but not at the Little Lake, and there were diving boards and towers and beauty pageants at the smaller lake.[7]

On Labor Day, September 1903, the Big Lake with suitable festivities was opened to all residents to show how Thurber's "Big Shots" spent their leisure time. This event was supposed to detract from union activities scheduled at Lyra, a UMW coal mining town five miles northwest of Thurber.[8]

In the valley below the Big Lake dam, truck gardens were sub-irrigated by seep water from the lake to provide Thurber with ample vegetables.[9]

"On the morning of January 24th, 1919, the northeast corner of the lake dam gave way following a night of hard rain...Fifty or sixty men were soon on the job with lumber and sand bags so about 1/3 of the lake water was saved ... the valley between the Lake and Mingus was full of fish."[10]

The two big silos about 200 yards to the east of Big Lake were built in 1919 to store silage for the Company's dairy cows and slaughter cattle.[11] The Thurber Dairy was established in 1895 but was closed in 1921 after coal mining was curtailed.[12] A slaughter house was built north of Thurber where beef and pork were processed. While most slaughter cattle came from company range, it was often necessary for the Company's cattle buyers to buy hogs and cattle from farmers and ranchers in Thurber's vicinity.[13]

THURBER'S DRY GOODS STORE

This building housed the Dry Goods and Furniture Store and the undertaker. It was a part of Texas Pacific Mercantile and Manufacturing Co. (T P M & M Co.), a subsidiary set up in 1894 to manage Texas and Pacific Coal Co. stores, saloons, Opera House and other commercial enterprises.[1]

With T P M & M Co., the coal company offered "Service from Cradle to Grave." One was born in a company house, attended by a company doctor, fed and clothed from company stores, educated in a company school, and entertained by company recreational activities and facilities. As an adult, one was employed by the company, married in a company church building, domiciled in a company house, with company utilities, and furnished with furniture and house wares from company stores. And at death the company mortician would arrange for burial in a company casket at the company cemetery.[2]

In 1889 T & P Coal Co. President R.D. Hunter built a barbed wire fence around Thurber and armed guards patrolled the fence. Thurberites believed the fence prevented them from buying outside and kept farmers and merchants from selling inside Thurber.[3] The 1903 Miners' Strike forced the removal of the fence and folks could then freely trade outside Thurber.[4] Company stores were stocked with variety and quality goods found only in the finest stores.[5] T P M & M Co. also had a large general store on Polander Hill where Italians, Poles and Mexicans could conveniently shop.[6]

T P M & M Co. "check" (scrip or coupons) were sold in books from $1.00 to $10.00 and this was accepted as money in saloons and stores. Employees could buy "check" books on credit, but once enmeshed in the "check" system, it was difficult to earn enough cash to meet needs of the coming month. The "check" system ensured that most all earnings were spent in company stores, the only places where "check" was accepted.[7]

SNAKE SALOON NOTES

1. Weldon Hardman, **Fire in a Hole!**, Gordon: Thurber Historical Assn. 1975, p. 95.

2. Ibid.

3. Sergeant W. J. L. Sullivan, **Twelve Years in the Saddle**, Austin: Von Boeckman-Jones, 1909, p. 35.

4. Mary Jane Gentry, Thurber: "The Life and Death of a Texas Town," Austin: Master's Thesis, University of Texas, 1946, p. 71.

5. Ibid. p. 70.

6. Ibid. p. 69-70.

7. Ibid. p. 76.

8. Hardman, p. 95.

9. Ibid.

10. Ibid.

11. Ibid. p. 96.

12. Ibid.

13. Ibid.

14. Ibid.

15. Gentry, p. 158.

16. Ibid. p. 130.

17. Ibid.

18. Leo S. Bielinski, The Back Road to Thurber, Baird: Joy Presswork Collection, 1993, p. 162.

19. Leo S. Bielinski, "Beer, Booze, Bootlegging and Bocci Ball," Abilene: West Texas Historical Association Yearbook, Vol. LIX, 1983, p. 78.

THURBER CEMETERY NOTES

1. Leo S. Bielinski, "Location of Graves in Thurber Cemetery", Thurber: Unpublished, Author's personal files, January 1993, East Section p. 1.

2. Faye and Butter Bridier, "Thurber Cemetery Memorial Listing," Thurber: Unpublished, Author's personal files, December 1992.

3. People were careful to observe unwritten rules and bury in appropriate section of cemetery.

4. Leo S. Bielinski, "Location of Graves", East Section, p. 2.

5. Mary Jane Gentry, "Thurber: Life and Death of a Texas Town," Austin: Master's Thesis, University of Texas, 1946, p. 148.

6. Leo S. Bielinski, "Thurber, Texas. Demise of Thurber Cemetery and Interments", Gordon: Thurber Historical Association, April 1990, p. 4.

7. Rosalie Salazar, age 83, Strawn, Texas. Several interviews summer 1992.

8. Leo S. Bielinski, "Location of Graves," North Section p. 1. Gineata, Libera and Pierino Castaldo; Mori Gennaro 15, 1919, Gennaro 15, 1919 and Gennaro 22, 1919; respectively.

9. Rev. O. A. McBrayer, Santo, TX: Unpublished research paper on Rev. Dodson, 1993.

10. Leo S. Bielinski, "Location of Graves", Center Section, p. 2.

11. Abilene Reporter News, "Dreams of a New Life Sleep Here", June 21, 1993.

GORDON HOUSE NOTES

1. Weldon B. Hardman, Fire in a Hole! Gordon, Texas: Thurber Historical Association, 1975, p. 19.

2. Who's Who in America, 1936-1937 ed., Vol. 19, Chicago: A. N. Marquis Co., 1937, p. 1,010.

3. Boyce House, Were You in Ranger?, Dallas, Texas: 1935: and Oil Boom, Caldwell, ID: Caxton Printers Limited, 1941.

4. Jay C. Henry, University of Texas at Arlington, School of Architecture, letter describing Gordon House, October 14, 1994.

5. Raymond Bridier, Mansfield, Texas: Interview October 1994.

6. Willie M. Floyd, "Thurber, Texas: an Abandoned Coal Field Town," Dallas: Southern Methodist University, Master's Thesis, June 1939, p. 40.

THURBER'S OPERA HOUSE NOTES

1. Mary Jane Gentry, Thurber: Life and Death of a Company Town, Austin: M.A. Thesis, University of Texas, 1946, p. 164.

2. Texas Mining and Trade Journal, Thurber: October 24, 1896.

3. Leo S. Bielinski, The Back Road to Thurber, Baird, TX: Joy Presswork Collection, 1993, p. 18.

4. Ibid. p. 185.

5. Weldon Hardman, <u>Fire in a Hole!</u>, Gordon: Thurber Historical Association, 1975, p. 120.

6. Gentry, p. 177.

7. C. Richard King, "Opera Houses in West Texas", Abilene: West Texas Historical Association Yearbook, Vol. XXXVIII, 1962, p. 101.

8. Gentry, p. 165.

9. Hardman, p. 120.

10. Dan Gentry, Dallas: Interview 18 September 1994.

11. Historical Edition, <u>Fort Worth Mail Telegram</u>, "The Thurber Mines," 14 May 1896.

12. Southern Living, October 1979. <u>Dallas Morning News</u>, Frank Tolbert, "Texas," July 6, 1966.

13. Hardman, p. 120.

14. Dan Gentry Interview.

15. Hardman, p. 120.

16. George B. Studdard, Life of the Texas Pacific Coal and Oil Co., 1888-1963, Fort Worth: 1993, p. 81.

HOTEL KNOX NOTES

1. <u>Texas Mining and Trade Journal</u>, Thurber: February 27, 1898.

2. Historical Edit. <u>Fort Worth Mail-Telegram</u>, "Thurber Mines", May 14, 1896.

3. Weldon Hardman, <u>Fire in a Hole!</u>, Gordon, TX: Thurber Historical Association, 1975, p. 104.

4. Ibid.

5. Mary Jane Gentry, "Thurber: the Life and Death of a Texas Town", Austin: Master's Thesis, University of Texas, 1946, p. 150.

6. Ibid.

7. <u>Fort Worth Star Telegram</u>, Ed Brice Column, Date unknown, perhaps 1980s. Copy in Bernice Bearden's File, Mingus, TX 76463.

8. Texas Mining and Trade Journal, Thurber: Reprint from Texas Farm and Ranch Magazine, "Pioneer Texas Industry", October 1, 1898.

9. Mary Jane Gentry, p. 152.

10. Historical Edition, Fort Worth Mail-Telegram.

11. Willie Floyd, "Thurber, Texas, an Abandoned Coal Field Town," Dallas: Master's Thesis, Southern Methodist University, June 1939.

12. George Studdard, Fort Worth: Interview September 13, 1994.

ST. BARBARA'S CHURCH NOTES

1. Leo S. Bielinski, "St. Barbara's Church at Thurber", Polish Genealogical Society of Texas News, Vol. VIII, No 3, Fall 1992, Houston, p. 12.

2. Baptismal Records (1893-1942) On file at St. Rita's Church, Ranger, TX. Also, Fact Sheet St. Barbara's Thurber, TX, Diocese of Dallas Archives to Dan Gentry, Dallas, Dec. 1993.

3. Weldon Hardman, Fire in a Hole!, Gordon, TX: Thurber Historical Association, 1975, p. 117. Fact Sheet Dallas Diocese to Dan Gentry.

4. Dallas-Fort Worth Diocese Information Sheet on St. Barbara's, July 19,67, author's personal file.

5. Benedictine Monks, St. Augustine's Abbey, Ramsgate, The Book of Saints, Wilton, Connecticut: Morehouse Publishing, 1989, p. 74.

6. St. Barbara's Baptismal Records.

7. Ibid.

8. Dallas Morning News, September 14, 1903.

9. As recalled by Joe Daskevich on several occasions.

10. Mary Jane Gentry, "Life and Death of a Texas Town", Austin: MA Thesis, University of Texas, 1946, p. 161.

11. Weldon Hardman, p. 116. Lottie Wasieleski Bielinski Interview June 1985. Lottie attended Hunter Academy from 1904-1913.

12. Dallas-Fort Worth Diocese Information Sheet.

13. Baptismal Records.

14. Dallas Diocese Archives. The saw cut is still visible in the Church today.

15. Mary Auda Franks Interview June 1985. According to Dan Gentry, Dallas, December 1993, the alcove was originally built to place a few statues in this space, but this was never done.

16. Baptismal and Interment Records, St. Rita's Church, Ranger, TX.

17. Mary Auda Franks. Church bell could be heard three miles on a quiet day.

NEW YORK HILL NOTES

1. Weldon B. Hardman, Fire in a Hole!, Gordon, Texas: Thurber Historical Association, 1975, p. 103.

2. Ranger, Texas Chamber of Commerce, sign on I-20 east of Ranger.

3. George Carter, "The Thurber Story, Part 6", Strawn Tribune, Strawn, Texas, (date unknown, copy in author's collection).

4. Willie Floyd, "An Abandoned Coal Field Town", Dallas: SMU Master's Thesis, 1939, p. 89.

5. Weldon Hardman, p. 102.

6. Edgar Marston to I. C. Van Noy, ltr May 8, 1918. (copy in author's collection).

7. John Boyd Harlin, "PROGRAMME", Thurber Club New Year's Eve Dance, December 31, 1931.

8. Mrs. Calloway Costa Interview June 1990. At the age of seventeen Mrs. Costa was thrilled to dance with Lawrence Welk at the Thurber Club.

9. Willie Floyd, p. 100.

10. Mrs. Mike Bertino, Mingus, TX Interview April 1988. Mrs. Bertino still lives in House #925 which was moved from New York Hill.

FIRST COAL MINE NOTES

1. S. M. Greenidge, "Report on Coal Reserves of T & P Coal and Oil Co.," Dallas: T & P Oil Co. Dec. 1953, p. 16.

2. Robert W. Spoede, "William Whipple Johnson: an Enterprising Man," Abilene Master's Thesis, Hardin-Simmons University, 1968, p. 53.

3. DVD "Boom Town to Ghost Town," Gordon, TX: Thurber Historical Association, 1988.

4. Leo S. Bielinski, The Back Road to Thurber, Baird, TX: Joy Presswork Collection, 1993, p x.

5. George Green, "Transcribed Interview with Mr. Lawrence Santi," Arlington: University of Texas at Arlington, Oral History Project, Texas Labor Archives, 1974, p. 5.

6. Weldon Hardman, Fire in a Hole!, Gordon, TX: Thurber Historical Association, 1975, p. 64.

7. Bielinski, p x. Richard Mason, DVD "Boom Town to Ghost Town."

8. Hardman, p. 56.

9. Greenidge, p. 16.

10. Spoede, pp. 54, 76, 101, 115, 144, 146, 149

THURBER BRICK PLANT NOTES

1. Glen Ely, DVD "Boom Town to Ghost Town", Gordon, Texas: Thurber Historical Association, 1991.

2. Weldon B. Hardman, Fire in a Hole!, Gordon, Texas: Thurber Historical Association, 1975, p. 78.

3. Ibid., p. 79.

4. Ibid.

5. Roland McMinn, "Thurber Brick and Their Makers", Lake Orion, MI: Journal Brick Collectors Association, Spring 1984, p. 50.

6. Leo S. Bielinski, Personal Brick Collection, Mingus, TX. LaClede Bricks can be found at the site of former Brick Plant.

7. Mary Jane Gentry, "Thurber: the Life and Death of a Texas Town," Austin: MA Thesis, University of Texas, 1946, p. 44.

8. Hardman, p. 80.

9.   Raymond Bridier, Mansfield, Texas: Interview March 1993.

10. McMinn, p. 49

11. Hardman, p. 78. Note: "Vitrified" means heated sufficiently to become glassified-like and non-porous to moisture.

12. Leo S. Bielinski, The Back Road to Thurber, Baird, TX: Joy Presswork Collection, 1993, p. 186. Union Brick Contract September 1914-1917, Thurber Brick Plant and BTT Local 153, Sec. 1, p. 1.

13. Hardman, p. 84.

14. Ibid.

15. Leo S. Bielinski. As a twelve-year-old, the writer could clean about 400 bricks a day; earning 60 cents.

16. Hardman, p. 85.

17. Bielinski, p. 150.

BIG LAKE NOTES

1.   Weldon Hardman, Fire in a Hole!, Gordon TX: Thurber Historical Association, 1975, p. 105.

2.   Willie Floyd, "Thurber Texas: an Abandoned Coal Field Town," Dallas: Master's Thesis, SMU, 1939, p. 39.

3.   Hardman, p. 106.

4.   Floyd, p. 39.

5.   Mary Jane Gentry, "Thurber: the Life and Death of a Texas Town", Austin: Master's Thesis, University of Texas, 1946, p. 175.

6.   Ibid. p. 175.

7.   Hardman, p. 124.

8.   Leo S. Bielinski, The Back Road to Thurber, Baird, TX: Joy Presswork Collection, 1993, p. 180.

9.   Hardman, p. 111.

10. George Carter, "The Thurber Story, Part III", Palo Pinto County Star, 1966. Copy in writer's personal collection.

11. Ibid. Part IV

12. Hardman, p. 111.

13. Hardman, p. 110.

DRY GOODS STORE NOTES

1. Mary Jane Gentry, "Thurber: the Life and Death of a Company Town," Austin: Master's Thesis, University of Texas, 1946, p. 105.

2. Weldon Hardman, <u>Fire in a Hole!</u>, Gordon, Texas: Thurber Historical Association, 1975, p. 90.

3. Ibid.

4. Leo S. Bielinski, <u>The Back Road to Thurber</u>, Baird, TX: Joy Presswork Collection, 1993, p. 185.

5. John Biondini and Mary Auda Franks, VCR "Boom Town to Ghost Town", Gordon, TX: Thurber Historical Association, 1988.

6. Gentry, p. 124.

7. Gentry, p 112.

INQUESTS INTO THURBER DEATHS

*T*here were few violent crimes in Thurber. Most "lockups" were for drinking or fighting. For the forty year span (1892-1932) the Erath County Justice of the Peace recorded only 40 inquests into Thurber deaths, 13 industrial accidents and 17 suspicious deaths. Of the suspicious deaths, only four could be clear cases of homicide. One inquest was that of John Cerwinski whose death was the subject of a previous story, "A Murder in Thurber", p. 102. Of the 11 mine accidents, five happened at No. 5 Mine.

The following information is from "Pathways to the Past" by Mildred Shirley and Jean Mansell with permission of Abilene Reporter-News, date unknown.

Killed in the mines of Thurber were:

1. J.G. Bailey, about 28, of light mulatto complexion, died March 31, 1893, being caught between the cage and the wall of Shaft No. 2.

2. Joe Cabbella, a 28-year-old Italian, died Dec. 5, 1893, in his bed after sustaining injuries in Mine shaft No. 5.

3. Robert Tweed, native of Scotland, died July 30, 1894, from injuries received while helping to sink Mine shaft No. 7.

4. R.H. Dawson, about 23, died Nov. 10, 1894, while working in Mine No.3.

5. J.M. Wilson, about 45, died Nov. 30, 1894, from injuries received by the falling of slate loosened by a shot fired by the deceased while brushing (clearing mine tunnel).

6. Thomas Shinder, 25, or 26, a native of Russia, died March 19, 1895, following an accident while working in mine No. 5.

7. F.M. Witherspoon, about 34, died June 24, 1895, after being crushed while helping to pole cars off No. 5 siding.

8. Fielding P. Ewing, 27, a resident of Breckenridge, died when he lost his footing and fell between the cars of the Thurber coal train.

9. Gus Poindexter died Nov. 23, 1895, near Mine shaft No. 5 when a coal car passed over him, crushing his skull.

10. Joe Borboum, 35, a Switzerland native, died June 18, 1896, when he was knocked from the cage down into the mine shaft as he was being hoisted out of Mine No. 5.

11. R. Guerra, a 23-year-old Mexican died Nov. 18, 1915, after a rock fell on him in Mine No. 3.

Two other work-related accidents:

12. Killed at the Green and Hunter Brick Company in Thurber was Dave Shannon, 32, who was caught in the belting which caused him to be crushed to death on March 6, 1900.

13. Walter Stanfill, 30, assistant engineer at the Thurber Ice Plant, was accidentally hit with a lever as he started up a machine, and for unexplained reasons was crushed to death.

Other deaths:

1. Joseph Del Belli, 30, died of gunshot wounds on Aug. 27, 1894.

2. Bart Gavin, 62, a Switzerland native, died Oct. 18, 1895.

3. Frederico Gatto, a 24-year-old Italian, died after being shot with a pistol Nov. 21, 1900.

4. Jospeh Pena, born July 17, 1880, in Mexico, was shot twice and cut with a knife to the temple by two Assailants May 19, 1907.

5. Guseppe Rinaldo, a 31-year-old Italian, committed suicide by shooting himself with a 12-gauge shotgun Oct. 18, 1907.

6. Simon Villanueva, about 38 and a native of Mexico, had his skull crushed by a blunt instrument by an assailant Nov.10, 1908.

7. George Bobolotto (Bokolotto), about 23 and a native of Italy, died of alcoholism Dec 25, 1912.

8. Salvatore Silapo, 30, a southern Italian, was shot by a pistol on Jan. 1, 1912.

9. Victor Sosnowski, about 60, drowned at the Little Lake in Thurber on March 29, 1912.

10. John Cerwinski, about 25 and a native of Russia-Poland, was stabbed through his heart May 26, 1912.

11. Jawdochia Macelinch, 33, born in Austria, committed suicide by taking poison Aug. 17, 1912.

12. Antonio Geramini, 61, born in San Martino Italy, burned to death in his home Feb. 17, 1913. Cause of fire was not determined.

13. Adolf Krupovich; 35, born in Okolibza, Russia-Poland, drowned in the No. 3 Mine lake on July 9, 1913.

14. Seon-Leon Vichorick, 45, a Polish man, committed suicide by poisoning on Oct.3, 1913.

15. Stanislaw Kaszycki, 37, born in Austria, "cut his throat while in a calaboose," Dec. 30, 1913.

16. Steve Millinch died between November 1915 and December 1920. No other information is available.

17. Pietro Maraschin died of heart failure between November 1915 and December 1920. (Obviously, dates for the last two entries are in error.)

GORDON BAINES RECALLS THURBER
PEOPLE AND EVENTS

Shortly before he passed on, Gordon Baines made a list of over 400 Thurber employees and where they worked. This covered a twenty year period from about 1910 to 1930. Coal miners were not included on this list, and with the exception of painters, carpenters, brick workers and ranch workers, most of the names were "white collar" workers who worked downtown in the stores and offices. This was an exceptional feat of recall in itself, but Mr. Baines also added a few other reminiscences.

Mr. Baines was born in Thurber in 1897 and his first job in Thurber was as a delivery boy for the Grocery Store on Polander Hill which he referred to as "600 Hill." Note that some workers shifted about in various positions. This many office workers were another indication of the operational extent of a Company Town which boasted of services from "Cradle to Grave." With many downtown workers unmarried, it is easy to understand the necessity of Boarding Houses: Hotel Knox, Marston Hall, Mrs. Plummer and Mrs. Masters. Most of the married downtown workers lived in brick bungalows on Marston Avenue.

EARLY DAYS OF COALVILLE

First train roped by Jeff Cowden near Gordon, Texas in 1881. Early mines furnished coal for T & P trains. The Coalville camp had a population of several hundred. A few miles north of Gordon, along the west side of Clayton Mountain coal cropped out in many places for about a mile. It was most noticeable at the foot of the mountain, but not in a large amount.

First mine by James, Cowan and Nolan in 1881 was a drift mine into the west side of the mountain; called the Gordon Mine. Mining begun just before the rails reached Gordon. A coaling table was built west of Barton Creek. Berry was the Foreman. Wagons hauled the coal here and coal was loaded into rail cars.

Charlie Finnigan was the first Superintendent of Coalville mine. After two years the camp grew to a town of several hundred. Demand for fuel grew and coal expansion demanded another mine (#2) about ½ mile south of #1. The town had tripled in size in two years and water shortage became a problem. Homes used wooden barrels filled with water hauled to them in a cypress wood tank at five cents per barrel.

In 1887 a drought hit the area. There was a crop failure and the Red Cross shipped in corn.

W. W. JOHNSON

W. W. Johnson sunk the first coal mine in northern Erath County in 1886. Everyone watched and waited. He had a crew cutting post in the cedar brakes. His crew, the Carlisle brothers, dug into hard shale just south of what later became the Brick Yard. The shale was hoisted by a mule. Finally, at 65 feet coal was hit but it took a longtime to develop the mine. Johnson also started the New Castle Mine which was about a mile south of his first mine. But this mine never fully developed. Next, he opened up Mineral City #1 which he later sold to Strawn Coal Co. He later developed the Rock Creek Mine east of Mineral Wells. He also started the Mt. Marion Mine at Strawn.

He bought the John Bird League north of Gordon and retired to this ranch. With a number of improvements he spent several years building houses, barns, fences, a deer park and a large lake. He and his family are buried in a mausoleum on the ranch.

THURBER SMOKESTACK

Built in 1908. Structural work by Gus Holmes, E. Marrs and Warren Wiggins. A timber broke, Holmes fell 20 feet. Broke ribs and was in bad condition for a long time. Some of the brick layers: Minton DaLee, Charlie Hamilton and Brewer.

STORE OFFICE

Ed Britton
F. D. Bostaph
Matt Williams
Mose Miller
J. E. Buchanan

LUMBER YARD

Jerry Dishroon
Aaron White
K. C. Jones
Woods (ball pitcher)
Allen Dishroon

DEPARTMENT MANAGERS

J. H. Whitmer,	Brickyard
Joe Watson,	"
J. Eaton,	"
J. H. Reeves,	Drugstore
Smith,	"
Wheat,	"
George,	"
Wynn,	"
Durden	"
M. M. Miller,	Dry Goods
Barnes,	"
Orb Barrett	"

GENERAL OFFICE

Lefty Adkins
Leo Miller
Frank Miller
Roy Miller
Clarence Davis
Pete Currin
Del Masso
Lonnie King (pitcher)
Rita Criswell
Welty Criswell
Frank Martin
Shaw

W. M. Creighton,	Grocery
J. E. Latimore,	Market
J. E. Lee,	Ice Plant
A. Davenport,	Hardware
George Taylor,	"
J. A. Terbet,	Machine Shop
R. T. Hume,	Stable
Frank Whitworth,	Blacksmith
Ed Lockhart,	Garage
V. E. Gustavis,	Gen. Store
J. D. Miller,	Housing
Jerry Dishroon,	Saloon
A. White,	Lumber Yard
K. C. Jones,	"
Mr. Woods,	Ball Pitcher

CLEANERS

Mr. Mowery
Deanrond Mowery
Myrtle Mowery
Oliver Crane
Brown

DRY GOODS

J. E. Barnes
Capt. Ready
Orb Barrett
Sam Ready
Jim Smith
John Melford
Mr. Wells
C. C. Cochran
Mr. Jobe
Mr. Franks
Lottie Davenport
Lena Bowers
Delores Angus
Mrs. Hennegar

Allan Dishroon
George Pinkston
Clint Kimbro
Bill Creighton
Dean Hyatt
Mr. Willettt
Noyes Willett
Eldon Willett
Bill Merritt
Matt Merritt
Frank Whitworth
Dean Bowers
Ray Bowers
Brant Holmes
George Paulowsky
Lona Kimbro
George Updike
Vasti Goldsmith
Hazel Creighton
Maurice Willett
Rocky Rhoades
Lura McLure
Bates Cox
Guy Randle
Everett Gibson
Loyce Gibson
O. E. Mitchell
R. S. King
Cliff Patterson
Ray DeCordova
Jessie DeCordova
L. D. Smith

BLACKSMITH

Frank Warholich
Bill Davis
Bill Fuller
Ira Hawkins
Roscoe Black

Marge Terbet
Phil Bowers
Bob Rodgers (Porter)
J. E. Pratt
Mr. Ajares

POST MASTERS

Frank S. Cronk	May 20, 1889
Walter Ready	June 20, 1893
W. K. Gordon	Apr 21, 1894
Thomas Guthrie	Mar 28, 1891
Lottie Guest	Dec 29, 1912
William Boyd	July 25, 1913
John Plummer	Mar 29, 1922
Oscar Weaver	Mar 23, 1934
Faye Nichols	Apr 30, 1936
P. O. closed	Apr 30, 1936

GROCERY STORE

Wm. Creighton, Mgr
Vic Creighton
Allen Dishroon
Jerry Dishroon
Jim Crane
Henry Latimer
Haney Poyner
Alpha Clark
Mart Livingston
Andy Patterson
Herbert Phelps
Daisey Varley
Jack White
Chas. DeWitt
Lurlyn Woodall
Jim Carlyle
Bill Creighton

GENERAL STORE ON 600 HILL (POLANDER HILL)

V. E. Gustavis
Leslie Jordan
Leslie Roberts
Doc LaGrone
Cicero Harris
Pete Vietti
Bart Bartino (Band Dir.)
Gordon Baines

OLD SCHOOL (Old Brick Saloon) 1904-1906 Teachers

Prof. Chastain
Mrs. Russell
T. W. Windle
Faye Hennegar
Mae Kelley

NEW SCHOOL TEACHERS

T. A. Parker
Faye Hennegar
Mrs. Russell
Mrs. T. W. Windle
Mr. Smith
H. B. Brown
Mr. Castivius
Olive Hopkins
Edith Creighton
Minnie McFarland
Mattie Lake
Mabel___
Eva Brackeen
Wynne Smith
Alvin Smith
Edith Dishroon
Pearl Martin

Doc LaGrone
Jim Farr
Rue Dorris
Isom (Negro
Grant helpers)
Frank Conn
Joe McKinnon
Lottie Guest

LABOR DAY QUEENS
Nell Carter
Jessie Carter

CO. OFFICIALS
R. D. Hunter
H. K. Thurber
Jerome Kerby
W. K. Gordon
J. W. Knox
R. S. King
Ed Britton
Mart Williams
Tom Hall
M. M. Miller
Tess McHarg
R. D. Bostaph
M. Farnsworth
R. D. Ratcliff

CARPENTERS
A. H. Miller, Mgr
J. D. Miller, Mgr.
Kilgore, 1st Mgr. built his house
(#108), on Brick Row
Frank Miller
Orb Rutherford
Raleigh Kenny
J. H. Howard
H. Stephens
J. E. Marrs

Freda Martin
Lyman E. Forrest
Francis Witcher
Mildred McCorkle
Miss Kopp
Helen Marrs
Bess Carter
Grace Easter
Gladys Pensor
Mary Caro

MINING OFFICE
J.E. Vamilyar
Tess McHarg
Roy Miller
J.D. Miller
Bill V__
J.E. Buchanan
Pete Vietti
Tom Jordan
Tom Hall
Cecil Swank
Clarence Davis
Forest Chisolm
Mutt Hartung

GARAGE
Ed Lockhart
Brant Pepes
Berlyn Dorris
Red Perry
BRICK YARD
J. H. Whitmer, Mgr.
Doc Woods
John Eaton
Joe Watson
Sam Hickman
Bill Hickman

Warren Wiggins
Gus Holmes
Bill Boyd
George Porter
SALOON
Jerry Dishroon
Imn Crane

OPERA HOUSE-PICTURE SHOW
Gus Peterson
Pete Gerhard
Bill Roberts
Chas. Hamilton
Roy Miller

HOTELS
Chinaman, 1st Hotel
Knox Hotel burned in 1907.
      Boarding House then built
      west of Mining Office.
Mrs. C. W. West, Mgr
Mrs. Plummer, Mgr
Mrs. A. S. Masters, Mgr

MEXICAN RESTAURANT
Ruiz & Magger, (on Thurber Jct.
      Road near Grocery Store)

SHOE SHOP
Frank Bida
Steve Bida
Frank Lenzini

TELEPHONE OFFICE

Mitchell
Cicero Harris
Lucy Oyler

Lee Magrew
Warren Kelley
Bert DaLee
Minton Lee
Bob Dorris
Tom Woods
Bob Jeter

OLD DRUGSTORE
J.H. Reeves, Mgr.
Tommie Jones
Gladys Jones
Sadie Nichols

NEW DRUGSTORE

J.H. Reeves
Mr. Smith
Mr. Wheat
Dr. Keith
Sadie Davidson
Mamie Kirkland
Joe Kimbro
Mr. Durden
Barney Hale
Lewis Ivey
Harvey Waters
Gladys West
Dollie Belle Harris
Shelton Gorhard
Jessie Mac Harris
Mr. George
Sadie Markland

BAKERY
Bill Butcher
Vic Creighton

FIRST MEAT MARKET, across from

Miss ____   lumber yard near Blacksmith and Stable

RANCH

W.F. Hayden, Mgr.
Mitch Hawkins
Geo. Bowers
Maye Wooten
John Bratton
Ben Dorris
Allen Eberhart
Virgil Hawkins
Dan Ince
Walter Coleman
Bill Reed
Tom Tibbs
Kerby Dorris
Brown (Negro Helper)

LIVERY STABLE

R.F. Hume, Mgr.
Frank Whitworth
Dixie Fenner
Bob Fletcher
Bob Freeman
Arthur Freeman
Calip Roberts
H. C. Martin
Geo. Bowers
Lon Gibson
Applegate
Lawrence Kitchens
Bill Kitchens
T.E. Patton
Newt Jones
Qulla Cole
Bill Roberts
Jim Williams
Gus Cramer
Allen Eberhart

BARBERSHOP

Dick Goodman
Tom Henley
Bill Carlyle
Bruce Henley
F.A. Garrett
Felix Davidson
Geo. Robbins
Dan Shamnessee

BRICK LAYERS

Mr. Brewer
Minton DaLee
Chas. Hamilton
Carl Roberts

PAINTERS

J.H. Beasley
Geo. Beasley
Henry Beasley
Tutt Whitworth
John Jordon
Les Jordon
Martin Patterson
Andy Patterson
Hoss Turner

DOCTORS

Binney
Dorsett
Baldridge
Holcomb
Petiqrew
Garlmo (Italian Dr.)
Shackleford

Keith

MACHINE SHOP
Luther Simmans
J.A. Terbet
Bill Terbet
John Terbet
Clarence Plummer
Oliver Thomas
Dick Thomas
Dominick Kessler
Campbell Bennie
Mart Anderson
Roscoe Black
Rue Dorris
Frank Conn
Bill Harmon

HARDWARE

Lon Davenport, Mgr.
Geo. Taylor
Bill Christian
Carl Snapp
John Kimbro
Joe McKinnon
Geo. Bowers
Ollie Waynick
Myrtle Edwards
Ine Turner

LAW ENFORCEMENT

Tutt Humes,	Jim Crane
Capt. Sawyer,	Harvey Hale
Capt. Johnson,	Bill Oxford
Bates Cox,	Geo. Hale
Bill Boyd,	Capt. Ready
Capt. Lightfoot,	Jim Southern

ICE PLANT
J.E.S. Lee, Mgr.
L. K. Ball, Mgr.
Butch Angus
J.E. Stanfield
Ind. Ivey
Cy Speigle
Bill Lorenz
Cotton Matthews
Bill Graham
Odie Freeman
Herbert Freeman
Jess Cheeks
Tutt Whitworth
J. C. Walker
Pete Gerhard
Frank Miller
Jim Williams
Rue Dorris

THURBER JOURNAL-PRINT

Mr. Brown, Editor
Boatright
Pauline Hull
Mr. Britton (Ed's Bro.)
Jack Harris
Elsie Marrs
Oscar Weaver
Walter McAdams
Mrs. Pinkerton

THE ITALIAN PRESENCE
IN THE COAL CAMP OF THURBER, TEXAS

The early coal mining settlements were called "camps" because when the coal vein played out, the miners moved to the next "camp." A membership ribbon of the Woodmen of the World Fraternal Lodge is stamped "Coal Camp No. 5, Thurber, Texas."[1] R. D. Hunter, president of Texas and Pacific (T & P) Coal Company at Thurber, in his "First Annual Report to Stockholders," referred to Thurber as "one of the most beautiful, quiet and healthy mining camps in the United States."[2] Forty years (1886 – 1926) was a long time for a camp to survive. In 1910 it was obvious Thurber would be far more than a mining camp because of its vast coal supply and the railroads' insatiable needs. Almost 13 million tons of coal was mined in Thurber, but 127 million tons remain.[3] Thurber had 16 mines (no more than four in operation at one time) and 20 miles of rails leading to the mines.[4] With a slaughterhouse, a cotton gin, and a market for farm produce, Thurber soon became an oasis for the farming and ranching area. By 1897 Thurber had a purified water supply, electricity, an ice plant, an opera house and a brick plant.

The hardworking, contented Italian work force must be credited for helping Thurber change from a camp to a modern city. Of the eighteen different nationalities in Thurber, the most populous of the foreign-born were the Italians who comprised 25% of Thurber's total population.[5] Significantly, the Italians made up about 52% of the coal miners, followed by the Poles with 12%, the Mexicans with 11%, and other Europeans 9%. The Irish, Scots, English, and Americans (including Blacks) comprised about 16% of the miners.

A feeling of family and home for young, homesick Italian miners was instilled by the hard work of the Italian wives when they cooked tasty Italian dishes for their boarders. An Italian family in Thurber would take in boarders for $18.00 a month. The wives, even with small children underfoot, prepared two full meals a day, a work lunch, and did laundry for the boarders. One family, the Constante Gruppos, had three children and eighteen boarders.[6] Boarding lessened the burden on the company to build extra housing, so this arrangement helped everyone. There were 927 Italians in 1910 Thurber, but today there are only four descendants in the area.[7]

While digging at a thirty inch layer of Thurber coal was an onerous task, it did provide an opportunity for many in repressed European countries. Underprivileged Italian youth were conscripted for dubious military campaigns. Sharecroppers and tenant farmers grubbed out a bare existence and there were few educational opportunities.[8] But the harshest blow was a government-imposed tax on grains which devastated the poor, whose main staple was bread. These conditions are outlined in a written account by Lorenzo Sartore. He worked a twelve hour shift in an Italian textile factory for the equivalent of twelve cents, USA.[9] The first Italian miners came to Thurber in response to advertisements in the northeastern mining regions of the U. S. Also letters, urging them to immigrate to America for economic and social reasons, were sent to cousins, brothers and nephews in northern Italy, and to villages in the foothills of the Alps.[10] Often passage money was enclosed in the letters. To illustrate this kinship, there were 23 Reginatos (men, women and children), 18 Serenas, 17 Dalbellos, 16 Biondis and 16 Andreattas in 1910 Thurber. Thus, only five families made up about 10% of Thurber's 927 Italians.

Thurber was not a Sicilian community, as one writer has referenced, because 95% of the Italians were from northern Italy.[11] Further, as Thurber grew, different ethnic groups tended to cluster. Following the railroad west from downtown Thurber, the first hill to the north of the track became "Italian Hill" and left of the track was "Polander Hill." Italian Hill was just inside the barbed wire fence which marked the northern boundary of Thurber.[12] Just outside this fence there were four Italian combination saloon and grocery stores: Mazzano, Ronchetti, Seaalfi and Corona.[13] These mom and pop stores stocked the different salamis, cheeses, pastas and olive oils needed for Italian cooking which were not available in the company store. The businesses were in Grant's Town, named for Jimmy Grant who first established a saloon just outside Thurber's barbed wire fence.[14]

The Italian mining force was a key determinant in the 1903 UMW unionization of Thurber. By 1889, a year after T & P Coal Company began operations, its president R. D. Hunter, had quashed the first union, the Knights of Labor, and for 14 years Thurber was an absolute open shop. Thurber miners worked for $1.00 per ton, ten hours per day, six days a week, and made about $35.00 a month. By 1903 the United Mine Workers (UMW) had organized miners in nearby Lyra (Strawn). Thurber's barbed wired fence kept out union organizers and the language barrier hampered organizers' efforts to communicate with the workers. However, since the Italians were the majority population, the UMW concentrated on these miners. Italian workers Gior Giuseppe, Peter Grosso and John Rolando were among the 14 signers of the union demands that initiated the 1903 Thurber Coal Miners Strike.[15]

Joe Fenoglio was sent in by the UMW to organize the Thurber Italian Miners.[16] He worked in the coal mines in Indian Territory before being sent to Thurber. It is not known where Joe Fenoglio went after his successful work in Thurber. Joe hired on as a miner in Thurber, but while on the job, and after hours, he fervently talked about the advantages of union membership. He feared that at any time the company could discover his intentions and manhandle him out of Thurber.[17] He quickly achieved his goal of uniting and igniting the Italian miners and quietly left Thurber.

Union organizational meetings had to be distanced from Thurber. The most impressive gathering was on September 10, 1903, at Rocky Creek Bridge (three miles north of Thurber) where the UMW from Lyra/Strawn marched two miles eastward to give support to several hundred Thurber miners. It was at this meeting that Tony Gardetto translated into Italian, French and Spanish the words of UMW national organizer W. M. Wardjon.[18] Tony Gardetto died in 1920 and is buried in the Thurber Cemetery.

The 1903 Thurber Coal Miners Strike was a consequential milestone for the labor movement in the southwest. Strikes were ineffective because management, often with government help, could kill a strike.[19] But after 1903, with Thurber now in the union fold and industry and transportation dependent on Thurber coal, labor unions held a decided advantage over employers. Thurber became a totally closed shop with every worker in Thurber belonging to one of several unions.[20] This was not a "Pyrrhic Victory," as one recent writer proclaimed, because it calmed the labor unrest among the miners, the company prospered and Thurber became a lively, modern community.[21] But there was one intra-union issue that persisted: the foreign-born miners made up 84% of the total mining force, but all UMW Local officials were Americans who made up only a small portion of Thurber's coal miners. These union officials ignored the grievances of the foreign-born miners and disregarded their religious holidays. In December 1906 at No. 9 Shaft, Frank Victtoria led a contingent of Italian miners who threatened to organize under the International Workers of the World (IWW).[22] The IWW was a socialistic, anarchist-leaning organization. And General Manager of Thurber W. K. Gordon could not tolerate this. As a result, Thurber became the only mining camp in America with two UMW Locals: the "Italian" Local No. 2753 and the original "English" Local No. 2538; the former being several times larger.[23]

Music was another Italian attribute which benefited Thurber. Many Italian miners had prior musical training, and combined with the innate musicality of the Italians, Thurber became a musical city. Every morning on Italian Hill wives would sing as they did Washing and ironing and baked bread in outdoor ovens. On weekends there were dances in the boarding houses or at the Italian Pavilion (the "Bearcat"), the Mexican dance Pavilion and the Polish Hall. On special occasions Lawrence Welk would appear at the exclusive Thurber Club.[24] Classical operas and school performances occurred at the Opera House. On Sunday evenings there were concerts at the bandstand. The sound of music pervaded Thurber with a dozen outstanding bands: the Hunter Band, the Thurber Band, the UMW Band, the Italian Band, the Tee Pee Band, the Stella d'Italia Band, the Mexican Band and others. Because of the ready pool of musicians in Thurber a band could be made up quickly for performances at nearby communities. Bart Bertino was maestro of the Italian Band. Dan Raffael was also a maestro in Thurber.

The Italians sought to acculturate themselves into the broader American society. Two ways that helped the process were to own land and join fraternal clubs. All land in Thurber was company land: 24,000 acres to the south, the east and the west. Thurber Junction was two miles north of Thurber along the main line of the Texas & Pacific Railroad. Mingus was north of the tracks and all the land, houses and businesses there were owned by Americans. South of the tracks was Thurber Junction with several Italian businesses: Santi Drug Store and paper route; Peretti's Garage and coal and ice; Auda Grocery; Taramino Grocery, a picture show, a dance hall, a saloon and wine bottling; Vietti Meat Market; Gazzola Furniture; Meneghetti Grocery and saloon; Lenzini Tavern and Rech Grocery and Feed.

In 1921 when the company evicted some miners for refusing to work at reduced wages, these miners and their families temporarily settled in "Tent City," an open field one mile north of Thurber. Here, they lived for eight months in World War I surplus tents. Lawrence

Santi, secretary of the Italian UMW Local, wheedled money from UMW headquarters to help the displaced families.

When the company began laying off miners in 1921, some turned to bootlegging as a means of livelihood. It was the Italians who were noted for their "grappa" (grape) whiskey. A story is told that a stranger asked a local resident where he could find some "home-brew." The resident said, "See that building with the flag? That's the post office. Then that brick building across the railroad tracks? That's the Baptist Church. Any place except those two buildings."[25]

By 1933 Thurber, once the most modern city between Fort Worth and El Paso, was being dismantled and/or moved away. Thurber's demise and the Great Depression caused most Italians to move to the coal fields in Illinois or to California. By 1950 the only indications of an Italian presence in the Thurber locale were the sumptuous, home-cooked Italian dinners at Lenzini's Tavern; Mrs. Biondini's Italian bread, mesquite-flavored, thick-crusted and still baked in an outdoor oven; and on weekends, the boisterous Italian bocce ball game played on outdoor courts that adjoined the saloons. Today, two bocce ball courts at the bottom of New York Hill are the only visible reminders of the Italian presence in Thurber.

THE ITALIAN PRESENCE NOTES

1. Hunter, R. D., "First Annual Report to Stockholders," Feb 19, 1893, Fort Worth, TX, (copy in author's collection), p. 4.

2. Display at New York Hill Restaurant, Thurber, TX.

3. State Historical Marker at the base of the Smokestack, Thurber, TX.

4. Gordon, W. K.," Data Submitted for T & P C Co. Twenty-Fifth Anniversary Souvenir," Thurber, Texas, July 4th, 1913, author, p. 6.

5. 1910, U S Census, Erath Co., Justice Precinct p. 7,

6. Ibid., p. 2B.

7. Interviews with Frances Solignani, Mary Zinanni, Rico Beneventi, and Amelia Biondini, author.

8. Bielinski, Leo S., The Back Road to Thurber, (Gordon, TX, Thurber Historical Assn, 2000), p. 107.

9. Sartore, Lorenzo, "Autobiographical Notes, Nov. 1984 – April 1985," author.

10. Leder, Frank T., Houston, TX. E-mail to Leo S. Bielinski, July 6, 2001, author. Research on Origins of Thurber Italians.

11. Rhinehart, Marilyn, "Underground Patriots: Thurber Coal Miners and the Struggle for Individual Freedom, 1888-1903," Southwestern Historical Quarterly, April 1989, p. 511.

12. Gentry, Mary, "The Life and Death of a Texas Town," M.A. Thesis, University of Texas, 1945, p. 13.

13. 1900, U. S. Census, Palo Pinto Co., Justice Precinct 3.

14. Hardman, Weldon B., Fire in a Hole!, (Gordon, TX, Thurber Hist. Assn, 1975), p. 35.

15. Dallas Morning News, Sept 11, 1903

16. Hardman, Fire in a Hole!, 47.

17. Ibid., p. 44.

18. Dallas Morning News, Sept. 14, 1903.

19. Green, George, "Transcribed Interview with Mr. Lawrence Santi," University of TX at Arlington, TX Labor Archives, 1974, p. 22. Use of Wisconsin National Guard in Milwaukee's Bay View Massacre, 5 May 1886. On four occasions R. D. Hunter, citing "threat of violence" from labor agitators, had Texas Rangers come to Thurber.

20. UMW, Brick Workers, Teamsters, Retail Clerks, Meat Cutters, Blacksmiths, Carpenters and Boiler Firemen.

21. Woodard, Don, Black Diamonds! Black Gold! (Lubbock, TX, Texas Tech Press, 1998), p. 84.

22. Gordon, W. K., Dec. 10, 1906 to Edgar L. Marston, Pres. T & P Coal Co., author.

23. Green, George, "Interview with Mr. Lawrence Santi," p. 18.

24. Studdard, George, "Life of the Texas Pacific Coal & Oil Co.," (Gordon TX, Thurber Historical Assn.) 1992, p. 114.

25. Gino Solignanni to Leo S. Bielinski, Interview Mingus, TX, Aug 1989.

THURBER STORIES BY GEORGE CARTER

*George Carter was born in Erath County in May 1882 and went to Thurber when he was about ten years old. He had many stories about Thurber and shortly before he died he wrote several articles at the request of his daughter Odessa Wylie. One of his stories is related previously in the chapter on **New York Hill**. It is fortunate that these stories exist because it gives a first hand account of what Thurber was, rather than what the later writers (revisionists) imagine Thurber should have been. George died in 1966 and is buried in the Thurber Cemetery. It is a privilege to reprint some of his stories which were published in the Palo Pinto Star newspaper in 1966.*

The entire Thurber Camp was fenced with six-foot-high barbed wire to keep out all peddlers of dry goods, groceries and all kinds of farm products. There were three gates, one on the south side, one on the west and one on the north. An old gray whiskered man, Captain Sawyer, rode these gates and believe me, nobody got past him. It continued that way for a long time and then the union organizers came in (1903). While they were trying to organize the coal miners in a union, the T. P. Coal Co. put armed guards on the coaches that carried the miners to coal pits each morning and returned each evening. Threats of violence were plentiful.

Among the guards were Captain Ready, Bill Oxford, Captain Lightfoot and Jack Larney. Finally the union was recognized and the high fence around the camp was taken down. Peddlers from everywhere flocked in with dry goods, groceries and farm products. The miners started on eight hour days with a wage raise.

Every man who worked the coal mines became union members as charter members and Thurber was really on the boom. New dwelling houses were erected and more coal miners were shipped in from as far away as Italy. Several different nationalities were represented although about 3/4ths of the miners were Italians. The Italians were a law abiding, fun loving lot of people and seemed to get lots of fun from an Italian wedding. The men were all good workers and excellent coal producers.

The coal pits varied in depth form 110 to 220 feet. A vein of coal was from 28 to 32 inches thick with a seam of cinders above the coal and below the coal vein.

In 1896 the Thurber Hospital was located about 100 yards northwest of where the big brick smokestack now stands. The hospital was a large frame building and well-equipped for a hospital at that time. Dr. Charles Binney was chief of staff and he was on duty day and night. Later, this hospital was replaced with a general doctors' office employing six doctors. The Company collected 50 cents per month from each worker and this entitled the worker and his family to all doctors' services for one month. However, when the union was recognized and wages went up, the doctors' fees were changed to $1.00 per month and later to $1.50 per month. When Thurber was abandoned, the fee had gone up to $2.00 per month. The coal company furnished each doctor with a good horse and buggy when Thurber was in its prime. These doctors were busy most of the day and night. The doctors were Binney, Pettigrew, Keith, Baldridge, Dorset and the Italian doctor Garlmo.

The Big Lake was dug in 1893. It took 50 men, one small steam shovel, four one mule dump carts, and two dump board wagons with mule teams. Two other mule teams, with long, heavy chains and two men to each team, drug away big logs and rocks.

The two big silos now standing about 200 yards east of Thurber Big Lake dam were built in the summer of 1917 to store silage for the T & P Coal Co.'s dairy cows and slaughter cattle. The company had a large herd of each kind. W. K. Gordon employed an expert dry land farmer, a Mr. Hayden. Several hundred acres of tillable soil was planted for silage in 1918 but only one silo was ever filled to capacity. Dry weather and other causes made the silage a failure. The silos were abandoned after two or three years of these failures. The early day Thurber dairy was located about 100 yards northeast of where the Thurber Big Lake is now located. There was a surface tank that covered about two acres when it was full of water. It was near the northeast corner of what is now the Big Lake and was at that time the only water supply for the dairy.

A fire broke out at 3 A. M. in 1892. There were 31 Jerseys and Holsteins in the big barn and the barn loft was full of hay. All the cows perished. The dairy was soon rebuilt on the same location.

In September 1896 I was spending the night with my late Uncle Jack Brewster in Thurber. Uncle jack was a hoisting engineer at the coal pits. Next morning we were awakened by all available whistles in Thurber (and the coal pits) blowing. Looking west we could see the big fire was at #5 coal pit about three miles away. Uncle Jack saddled his horse and I climbed on behind him. We took a short cut and it was a hard ride but we got to the fire at good daylight. A bunch of men had already formed a bucket brigade to a surface water tank about 60 yards away. Twenty seven men of the entire night crew were climbing up the steps of the man-way. They were a peculiar looking sight sticking their smoked black faces on top for fresh air and all dripping with water. The tipple, engine room and boiler room burned and seven mules perished at the bottom of the pit. Luckily though, there was no loss of life. (Note: The Mine Supt. J. H. McClure was awarded a gold medal by R. D. Hunter for McClure's heroism in leading the workers to safety.)

In 1903 a motor line from the Thurber brick yard was built one mile north to the rich shale pit mountain. The mountain line was graded by teams, wheel scrapers and slip scrapers. Then motor rails were put down on the length of the track. Shale from this mountain was used during the entire life of the brick yard. The workers grading this motor line were: Teamsters Will Lorenz, Bud Abbott, Joe Cates, Ed Patterson and George Carter. Bud Gibson and Wesley Earls filled the slip scrapers and wheel scrapers. The Rev. J. M. Earls dumped the slip scrapers and wheel scrapers. Rev. Earls was pastor of the Thurber Baptist Church. He dumped scrapers 10 hours a day and then held a prayer meeting at his church at night. (Not many preachers will do that.) Brother Earls was a good preacher and a wonderful man.

In six months the lake was filled with water and has never been entirely dry since then. Texas and Pacific put in a pipe line from Thurber about one mile to northwest corner of the lake dam and put a pump station near the dam. Then they erected a large cypress water tank on Cemetery Hill, near the north side of Thurber. A Mr. Bill Yates was the pumper at the station for several years. He used field glasses to see the outside gauge on the water tank.

On the morning of January 24, 1919 at 7:30 A. M., the northeast corner of the lake dam went out with a crash following a night of hard rain. Fifty or sixty men were soon on the job with lumber and sand bags so that about 1/3 of the lake water was saved. A motor line was put in from the west side of the lake across the dam to the east side where the break occurred. Motor and dump cars were used to haul dirt and rock across to the break. The electric power came from the brick yard. Several hundred sacks of cement with dirt and rock were used, so the northeast corner of the Big Lake dam should hold good for a long time.

The Thurber Lumber Yard had a large number of frame sheds, divided in sections to hold and protect several sizes and grades of lumber. Aaron White was manager of the yard. The carpenter shop was in the same enclosure. The Company generally kept eight or ten carpenters on the job. It took plenty of nerve to be a Thurber carpenter. Several times I have seen a carpenter; working at the top of a tipple over a mine shaft. If a cable had broken or a rope knot slipped, the carpenter would have fallen to the bottom of the pit, 200 feet or more. I remember seeing carpenters Forest Stevens and Green Bridges at the top of the tipple putting in the 18 and 24 inch bolts to hold the big timbers. It was just good luck that not a carpenter was ever seriously injured while at work in Thurber.

I was engineer at the Thurber ice plant from mid-summer of 1907 to mid-summer of 1909. The ice plant was located about 60 feet from where the big brick smoke stack stands today. The stack was built in the summer of 1908 so I witnessed the building of the stack. There were eight brick layers, four working inside and four working outside. The men were of different nationalities though all were expert brick layers. There were twelve scaffold builders and helpers and four mud makers. The big stack is a wonderful piece of brick building skill and will stand for many years.

I spent 18 months as the driver of the Thurber coal pulling "pit" mules. At the bottom of each coal pit was four entries, one from each direction. Usually at the east and west entrance was a mule stable capable of holding two to four mules each. The harness was made of heavy leather running from in front of the ears to halfway down the side and over the hips of the mules. This was to protect them from falling rock (slate). At the back was an attachment holding a 10-foot chain called the tail chain. The tail chain had a hook on the end for hitching onto pit cars and a heavy leather whip was always carried by the driver. These mules were trained to turn right when the driver said "gee" and to turn left on "haw."

At this time there was no electricity and the coal pits were pitch dark. The only light was from small lard oil burning pit lamp that hooked on the front of the pit cap. There was usually a 12 to 14-year-old boy, called a trapper, on each entry. About halfway between the face of the coal and the cage as at the bottom of the pit was a heavy curtain to hold in fresh air. The fresh air was furnished by a large fan at the top of the pit and circulated throughout. The trapper notified the driver of conditions by signs of his pit lamp. Straight up and down meant "all clear ahead, come on." A signal cross ways meant "don't come, wait." They also had several other signs the driver must obey. The mules knew the signs too and when the trapper gave the "go ahead" sign you'd better be ready for the next stop because the mule took off. A mule was always the first to detect trouble ahead. Usually it was a big piece of rock on the track. A pit mule is smart and usually knew more about coal pulling than the drivers did.

My last six months as a driver I used a mule named Clipper. My boss said not to try to pull more than three or four loaded cars at a time explaining that the mule was balky. The boss said I would need to put the whip to him. The next day I bought a dozen fresh apples, knowing how fond mules are of apples. Each day I cut one apple in four quarters, gave Clipper one when I arrived at the stable and gave him another quarter at the end of a heavy pull. I never used a whip on him and we brought in 12 to 15 loaded cars each trip. The apples got the job done. When I left that job to take another I regretted leaving Clipper to the heavy whip of the next driver.

TALES FROM GRAVE YARD HILL

The Thurber Cemetery was abandoned for 50 years (1940 – 1990). In spite of its unkempt condition and waist-high weeds, in 1967 this writer and a friend visited the cemetery for the first time in many years. Both of us had family buried therein. The cemetery is divided into three sections: Protestant, Catholic and African-American. Each section had its own entry gate. There were only a few burials in the cemetery during its abandonment. But when we visited the cemetery in 1967 we were surprised to see the mound of a new grave and a very large tombstone just to the right of the entry. This was in the African-American Section and the tombstone was the tallest in the cemetery. We knew practically everybody in the local area and many people who had lived in Thurber but we did not recognize the name on the monument. And the inscription was in error: "Killed in the Korean War, Jan 10, 1966." A check with funeral homes in Strawn, Ranger, Mineral Wells and Stephenville had no knowledge of this burial.

We visited the cemetery again a few years later and we were stunned to see that the grave and the monument had disappeared. What happened? Did the funeral home have the wrong cemetery by mistaking "Thurber" for a similar name? The plots in Thurber Cemetery had always been free to Thurberites and their relatives. Perhaps there was a disagreement over the error on the monument's inscription and the monument company was asked to remove the monument? Or, was the body re-interred in another cemetery? Are the remains still in Thurber cemetery?

The cemetery was restored in 1990. In 1993 a large granite "Lost Graves" memorial was set near the cemetery entrance. On the memorial there are over 700 names of those in unmarked graves. But in the whole cemetery only about 300 graves are identified.

211

Hundreds of inquiries have been about burials in the cemetery but none on African-Americans. Thus, it was another surprise when in early July 2008 someone had placed a white metal cross near the former grave of this service man "Killed in the Korean War, Jan 10, 1966." Who placed this cross? What did they know about this burial which took place in the late '60s? Although the tombstone was removed how did they know if the remains were still at this location?

Some lost graves in the Cemetery are located by scanning with two metal rods. There is a scientific explanation for movement of the metal rods and scanning has been used for many years in locating pipe lines, water lines etc. Scanning also determines the gender of a grave. Therefore, the area of the white metal cross was scanned and an adult male grave was indicated. But the metal cross identifying· the grave faced north and south when the grave was actually east and west. Movement of the scanning rods does not mean there is a grave, but rather that the soil has been disturbed. However, the gender indication by scanning was male. At the foot of this grave there was an indication of an infant's grave. So there are still questions.

SERENDIPITIOUS SALVATION ?

Some visitors to the Thurber Cemetery remark on the few Thurber deaths during the 1918 Spanish Flu epidemic. From Death Records on file at Erath County Courthouse the average number of deaths per year in Thurber was 17. But in 1918 only 16 deaths were reported. And in 1919 only 2 deaths! This strange anomaly is verified by Catholic Church Interment records which showed an average of about 9 deaths per year. However, Church records show only 8 deaths in 1918 and no deaths in 1919. Were the Churches, doctors, mortuary and families so over whelmed as to neglect reporting deaths? Could records keepers have been overcome by the volume of deaths at this time? Did folks just want this sad epic to be over with and forgotten?

In Thurber one remedy for the flu was an Epson Salt physic. The demand was so great that Epson Salt sold for $1. a tablespoon. In 1916 Erath County went "dry" and all the hard liquor in Thurber's Snake and Lizard Saloons was locked up, the notion being that the "dryness" would be short-lived. But in 1918 this whiskey cache was dispensed by doctors when flu symptoms were detected.

One possible explanation for the few 1918 – 1919 deaths is that the relatively high sulfur content of Thurber coal might have created an aseptic Thurber environment, thereby protecting Thurber residents from the Spanish Flu. Thurber coal contained over three percent sulfur. The miners were directly exposed to this sulfuric content. The Brick Plant and the Power Plant spewed sulfur-laden smoke over Thurber. There were the slag (mine tailings) dumps at each mine and walkways and roads and rail beds were made of slag. It has been noted that houses built on slag-leveled ground had no termites or cockroaches. In WWII sulfur drugs were widely used in treating wound infections and diseases. Were Thurber residents serendipitously provided flu immunity by a sulfuric environment from coal?

In a certain section of the cemetery, scanning indicated four parallel rows (trenches, indications of earth disturbance), each about 40 feet long and about six feet apart. Graves? The four "trenches" gave indications of burials, all male, but these burials were in a column, or tandem (rather than rows) and faced east. *Purely speculation.* Could this be evidence of mass burials? In any epidemic (1918 flu) there would be some deaths probably expected each day. Quickly get rid of the contamination. Accordingly, a "trench" would be much more convenient and easier work than digging individual graves each day. A "trench" might have been dug and the bodies placed in a single line (tandem). Each day a few more bodies were added. But if the bodies were placed too closely (head to feet) there might not be indications of individual burials. The only way mass burial could be verified would be exhumation but this would be extremely risky; for 1918 Spanish Influenza germs might still exist.

THE KNIGHTS OF PYTHIAS BURIAL PLOT

In the Cemetery there is a neat, brick walled plot about 18 by 36 feet. There was a Knights of Pythias symbol on the gate until someone made off with it. But this pleasant spot is a mystery because no one appears to be buried there. There is no knowledge about this plot, no markers and no grave indications.

The Knights of Pythias Lodges were active in this area until about 1940 but now the nearest K of P location is the K of P Home for Children at Weatherford, TX. But they could not provide any information on Thurber. The Grand Secretary, Pythias of TX, was contacted. He had no knowledge of a Knights of Pythias Burial Plot in the Thurber Cemetery but he did provide some interesting history of the lodge in the Thurber area. Yes, it was possible that this could have been a burial plot for K of P members; for each lodge had the ability to buy land for a cemetery. The Thurber Lodge was known as Diamond #159 and had 60 members in 1908. In 1929 the secretary pf this lodge was J. D. Miller and there were 46 members. The Diamond #159 merged with the Mingus Lodge #355 in 1935. Gordon had three K of P Lodges, #32, #54 and Enterprise #61. There were also Lodges in Santo, Ranger and Eastland. With so many Lodges around Thurber and such a prime burial site in the Thurber Cemetery it appears there should have been some burials in this plot; if not Lodge members, then perhaps family members.

In 2005 this plot was scanned with metal rods. Locating graves and gender by scanning has been tested, retested and verified by checking known graves and there is a scientific explanation for the movement of the rods. The rods are encased in the sleeves of a ball point pen and there is no contact with the scanner's hands. Scanning gave some astonishing results.

There were 15 graves in this 18 by 36-foot plot! All male adolescents save for two infants. All graves perfectly aligned, two graves in tandem, seven rows and all facing south. One could walk a two-foot wide, straight 36-foot long path between the two rows of graves. Could this be male sons of Lodge members? Why no tombstones? The Cemetery was abandoned for 50 years. Someone took the K of P medallion from the gate. Could someone have taken the tombstones which might have borne the K of P symbol?

THE ORIGIN OF THE THURBER GHOST

The story of a Thurber ghost has been around for a long time. Frank Tolbert of the Dallas Morning News resurrected this story in a May 15, 1983 article. The owner of the restaurant in Thurber was irritated because three of his employees had just quit because they claimed that Thurber had ghosts "in residence." "Two of the employees were a married pair of Cuban refugees, and the other was a 65-year-old maintenance man." These employees lived in apartments above the restaurant. The restaurant was in the bottom floor of the old two storied Thurber Drug Store. Tolbert also related that he had first heard of the ghost story in 1955 from Mrs. Eliza Whitehead who was one of the old-timers who had seen and heard a singing ghost. "I been here 40 years...I was just walkin' in downtown one night and here come this pretty woman singin' in some funny way. Then she just went away right in front of my eyes."

Thurber had an opera house and Thurber, with its large opera-loving Italian population, was a regular stop for touring opera companies. And Albert, Eliza's husband, was quoted: "You won't catch me passin' through town after dark."

Walter Kostiha and his brother Frank claimed to have seen the ghost. The Kostihas lived near the old jail house which was near downtown Thurber. Walter: "I don't care whether you believe me or not. I know what I saw, even if I was only about five years old. I was with my brother Frank behind the old grocery store, just about dark. We saw this woman in a white gown and she was singing or saying something. We took off running."

The Star Telegram (Oct 26, 1997) in a weekend Halloween edition did not help matters when they wrote "The Thurber Cemetery is one of the biggest of Texas' historical cemeteries. It is also one of the scariest places to be on a dark night. The trees bend over the graves as if in mourning for the 700 (sic) or more children buried there. The epidemics of scarlet fever and whooping cough…definitely left their mark on this Texas ghost town."

Raymond Bridier had a plausible explanation for the origin of the Thurber Ghost. When Raymond was about ten years old (say, around 1920), on moonlit nights a bunch of kids would meet at the ball park which at this time was on top of Graveyard Hill next to the cemetery. They would smoke cedar, play games like "kick the can" or just talk.

One night as they were going home, they noticed a lady in a white gown sitting on the top step of the sty (steps over the fence) in the southeast corner of the cemetery. She was crying or praying loudly, perhaps for a loved one she had recently buried in the cemetery. The kids thought this behavior odd but this quickened their pace toward home. The following night the same scene, but this time they took off running; something had spooked them. Now, they were afraid to play in the ball park after dark. But several weeks later courage had returned and they went back up the Hill. Nobody there.

They smoked and played their games, but as they exited the ball park and headed for home, she was there! She stood up on the steps and started toward them! They panicked and went tearing off down the Hill. They never did go back up to the ball park, and shortly thereafter, the ball park was moved to the east side of Thurber.

Thurber was virtually abandoned about 1935. People began calling it a Ghost Town, which was not true for there have always been several people living in Thurber. After this ball park episode which was a plausible event, all the alleged sightings have been in downtown Thurber. Some say the singing is caused by the wind whistling around the smokestack or through the old buildings. But Eliza Whitehead or Walter Kostiha would never believe that because they saw her with their own eyes and heard her.

Made in the USA
Lexington, KY
23 March 2012